AMERICA

BRIEF THIRD EDITION

STUDY GUIDE

Volume 2

TINDALL and SHI

AMERICA

A NARRATIVE HISTORY

STUDY GUIDE

BRIEF THIRD EDITION

CHARLES W. EAGLES
UNIVERSITY OF MISSISSIPPI

and

THOMAS S. MORGAN
WINTHROP UNIVERSITY

W • W • NORTON & COMPANY • NEW YORK • LONDON

ISBN 0-393-96372-1

W. W. Norton & Company, Inc.
500 Fifth Avenue, New York, N. Y. 10110
W. W. Norton & Company Ltd.
10 Coptic Street, London WCIA IPU

1 2 3 4 5 6 7 8 9 0

CONTENTS

INTRODUCTION

This *Study Guide* is designed to help you learn the important concepts in *America: A Narrative History,* Brief Third Edition, by George B. Tindall and David E. Shi. It is not intended as a replacement for the textbook, but as an aid to be used along with the text. When used conscientiously, this *Study Guide* will help you to understand the major themes in American history and to do well on quizzes based on your reading.

STRUCTURE OF THIS STUDY GUIDE

Each chapter of the *Study Guide* contains the following sections:

Chapter Objectives
Chapter Outline
Key Items of Chronology
Terms to Master
Vocabulary Building
Exercises for Understanding:
    Multiple-Choice Questions
    True-False Questions
    Essay Questions
Document(s) or Reading(s)

The purpose of each of the sections, along with instructions for its use, is explained below.

Chapter Objectives

For each chapter you will find about five objectives, or key concepts, on which you should

focus your attention as you read. You should read the whole of each chapter, taking in details as well as major themes, but by keeping the chapter objectives in mind you will avoid getting bogged down and missing the key ideas.

Chapter Outline

Skim this outline carefully before you begin reading a chapter. The outline provides a more detailed overview than do the objectives. Often headings in the outline are worded to suggest questions about the material. For example, "Duties of the King" and "Patterns of Colonization" raise the questions "What were the duties of the king?" and "What were the patterns of colonization?" Look for the answers to such questions as you read the text. This approach will help those of you who are new to reading history.

Key Items of Chronology

Each chapter of this *Study Guide* will include a list of dates. You need not learn every date you encounter in the chapter, but if you learn the key ones listed here and any other dates emphasized by your instructor, you will have the sound chronological framework so important for understanding historical events.

Keep in mind that dates, while important, are not the sole subject matter of history. Seldom will any of the quizzes in this *Study Guide* ask for recall of dates. On the other hand, term papers and answers to essay questions should include important dates and show that you are familiar with the chronology of your subject.

Terms to Master

This section of the *Study Guide* gives you a list of important terms to study. (Remember, of course, that your instructor may emphasize additional terms which you should learn.) After reading each chapter, return to the list of terms and write a brief definition of each. If you cannot recall the term readily, turn to the relevant pages in the textbook and reread the discussion of the term. If you need or want to consult another source, go to the annotated bibliography at the end of the relevant chapter, or ask your instructor for suggestions.

Vocabulary Building

This is a section of the *Study Guide* that you may or may not need. If you do not know the meaning of the words or terms listed in Vocabulary Building, look them up in a dictionary before you begin reading a chapter. By looking up such words and then using them yourself, you will increase your vocabulary.

When the terms in Vocabulary Building are not readily found in the standard dictionary or when their use in your text lends them a special meaning, we have defined them for you. We've used the *American Heritage Dictionary*, Second College Edition, as a guide to determine which terms should be defined here for you.

Exercises for Understanding

You should reserve these exercises to use as a check on your reading after you study the chapter. The multiple-choice and true-false questions included here will test your recall and understanding of the facts in the chapter. The answers to these questions are found at the end of each *Study Guide* chapter.

Essay Questions

The essay questions which come next may be used in several ways. If you are using this *Study Guide* entirely on your own, you should try to outline answers to these questions based on your reading of the chapter. In the early stages of the course you may want to consider writing formal answers to these essay questions just as you would if you encountered them on an exam. The questions will often be quite broad and will lead you to think about material in the chapter in different ways. By reviewing the essay questions in this *Study Guide* before attending class, you will better understand the class lecture or discussion.

Documents and Readings

All the chapters in this *Study Guide* contain a section of documents or readings. The documents are sources from the time period of the chapter (primary sources), chosen to illumine some aspect of the period covered in the text. The readings are excerpts from works of historians (secondary sources), chosen either to illustrate the approach of a master historian or to offer varying interpretations of an event. Study the document or reading after you have completed the chapter, and consult the headnotes given in this *Study Guide* before each document. Then attempt to answer the questions that follow the document.

STUDYING HISTORY

The term "history" has been defined in many ways. One way to define it is "everything that has happened in the past." But there are serious problems with this definition. First, it is simply impossible to recount *everything* that has happened in the past. Any single event is a combination of an infinite number of subevents. Each of these is itself composed of an unlimited number of subevents. The past, which includes everything that has happened, is shapeless; history is a way of lending shape to the past by focusing on significant events and their relationships.

Second, the historical record is limited. As

you will discover, there is much we don't know about everyday life in seventeenth-century America. History must be based on fact and evidence. The historian then, using the evidence available, fashions a story in which certain past events are connected and take on special meaning or significance. If we accept this definition, we will recognize that much history is subjective, or influenced by the perspective and bias of the historian attempting to give meaning to events.

This is why there is so much disagreement about the importance of some past events. You may have been taught in high school that it was important simply to learn dates and facts: that the Declaration of Independence was adopted on July 4, 1776, or that Franklin Roosevelt was inaugurated on March 4, 1933. But these facts by themselves are limited in meaning. They gain significance when they become parts of larger stories, such as why the American colonies revolted against England, or how America responded to the Great Depression. When historians construct stories or narratives in which these facts or events take on special significance, room for disagreement creeps in.

Since it is valid for historians to disagree, you should not automatically accept what any one historian writes. You should learn to apply general rules of logic and evidence in assessing the validity of different historical interpretations. This *Study Guide* will at times give you an opportunity to assess different interpretations of events. By doing this you will learn to question what you read and hear, to think critically.

HOW TO READ A TEXTBOOK

Reading a textbook should be both pleasurable and profitable. The responsibility for this is partly the author's and partly yours, the reader's. George Tindall and David Shi have written a text that should teach and entertain. In order to get the most out of it you must read actively and critically. One way to avoid passive, mindless reading is to write, underline, or highlight material by hand. Simply by highlighting or underlining pertinent passages in

the textbook, you will later be better able to recall what you have read and you will be able to review quickly important material. The key to effective highlighting is to be judicious about what you choose to mark. You should highlight key words and phrases, not whole sentences unless all the words are important. For example, the two paragraphs below show the way we would highlight them:

Even the Tudors, who acted as autocrats, preserved the forms of constitutional procedure. In the making of laws the king's subjects consented through representatives in the House of Commons. By custom and practice **the principle was established that the king taxed his subjects only with the consent of Parliament.** And by its control of the purse strings Parliament would draw other strands of power into its hands. This structure of habit broadened down from precedent to precedent to form a **constitution that was** not written in one place, or for that matter, **not fully written down at all.** The *Magna Carta* (Great Charter) of 1215, for instance, had been a statement of privileges wrested by certain nobles from the king, but it became part of a broader tradition that the people as a whole had rights which even the king could not violate.

A further buttress to English liberty was the **great body of common law** which had developed since the twelfth century in royal courts established to check the arbitrary caprice of local nobles. Without laws to cover every detail, judges had to exercise their own ideas of fairness in settling disputes. **Decisions once made became precedents for later decisions** and over the years a body of judge-made law developed, the outgrowth more of experience than of abstract logic. Through the courts the principle evolved that **a subject could be arrested or his goods seized only upon a warrant issued by a court** and that **he was entitled to a trial by a jury of his peers** (his equals) in accordance with established rules of evidence.

Probably no two persons would agree on exactly what words in the passage should be underlined, but you can readily see that we have emphasized only the major points concerning English justice.

Highlighting like this can be helpful, but even more useful in increasing your retention of the material is to jot down brief notes about what you read. For example, from the passage above you might list some key elements in the development of liberty under the Tudors: the principle that the king could tax his subjects only with the consent of Parliament, the development of an unwritten constitution, the principle that a court order was required for arrest or seizure of property, and the principle of trial by jury.

Taking notes makes it easier to commit important points to memory. This will help especially when you review for a test.

ACKNOWLEDGMENTS

We wish to thank George B. Tindall and David E. Shi for having written the excellent text around which we developed this *Study Guide*. Our hope is that the text and the *Study Guide* will combine to promote in students a clear understanding of the history of the United States. We have a great debt to Steven Forman, our editor at W. W. Norton & Company, who has again used his considerable skill to fashion the final product. He has created a unified revision from the different parts on which we each worked.

C.W.E.
T.S.M.

17 ✎

RECONSTRUCTION:
NORTH AND SOUTH

CHAPTER OBJECTIVES

After you complete the reading and study of this chapter you should be able to

1. Describe the impact of the Civil War on both the South and the North and on the status of freed blacks.
2. Explain the circumstances that led to Radical Reconstruction.
3. Describe the nature and extent of Radical Reconstruction.
4. Explain the process that returned control of the South to the conservatives.
5. Evaluate the contributions and failures of the Grant administration.
6. Explain the outcome of the election of 1876 and the effects of that election and the special arrangements made to conclude it.
7. Evaluate the overall impact of Reconstruction.

CHAPTER OUTLINE

I. Development of a plan of Reconstruction
   A. Military governors in Tennessee, Arkansas, and Louisiana
   B. Lincoln's plan of Reconstruction
   1. Provisions
   2. Implementation in Tennessee, Arkansas, and Louisiana
   3. Congressional reaction
   4. Counterclaims of Lincoln and Congress
   5. Wade-Davis Bill
   6. Lincoln's response to the Wade-Davis Bill
   7. Creation of Freedmen's Bureau
   8. Lincoln's final statement on Reconstruction

II. The assassination of Lincoln

III. Andrew Johnson and Reconstruction
   A. Johnson's background
   B. Radicals' perception of him
   C. Johnson's plan for Reconstruction

IV. Southern state reorganization
   A. Actions taken
   B. Congressional reaction to southern states
   C. Provisions and impact of black codes

V. The Radicals
   A. Joint Committee on Reconstruction
   B. Radical motivation
   C. Constitutional theories of status of southern states

VI. Johnson and Congress in battle
   A. Veto of Freedmen's Bureau extension

B. Effect of Johnson's Washington's Birthday speech
C. Congress overrides veto of the Civil Rights Act
D. The Fourteenth Amendment
E. Race riots in the South
F. The congressional elections

VII. Congressional Reconstruction triumphant in 1867
    A. Command of the Army Act
    B. Tenure of Office Act
    C. Military Reconstruction Act

VIII. Constitutional issues and the Supreme Court

IX. The impeachment and trial of Johnson
    A. Failure of early efforts to impeach him
    B. Violation of Tenure of Office Act
    C. The articles of impeachment
    D. The Senate trial
    E. Ramifications of the impeachment

X. Radical rule in the South
    A. Readmission of southern states
    B. Duration of Radical control
    C. Role of the Union League prior to Reconstruction
    D. Blacks in southern politics
      1. Characteristics of black control
      2. Extent of black control
    E. Carpetbaggers and scalawags
    F. Nature of new state constitutions

XI. Achievements of the Radical governments

XII. The development of white terror techniques
    A. Objections to black participation in government
    B. The Ku Klux Klan
    C. Enforcement Acts to protect black voters

XIII. The return of conservative control
    A. Reasons for abandonment of the Radical programs
    B. Duration of Radical control

XIV. The Grant years
    A. The election of 1868
      1. Reasons for support of Grant
      2. The Grant ticket and platform
      3. Democratic programs and candidates
      4. Results
    B. The character of Grant's leadership
    C. Proposal to pay the government debt
    D. Scandals
      1. Jay Gould's effort to corner the gold market
      2. The Crédit-Mobilier exposure
      3. Secretary of War and the Indian Bureau
      4. Other scandals
      5. Grant's personal role in the scandals
    E. Reform and the election of 1872
      1. Liberal Republicans nominate Greeley in 1872
      2. Grant's advantages
    F. Economic panic
      1. Causes for the depression
      2. Severity of the depression
    G. Democratic control of the House in 1874
    H. Reissue of greenbacks
    I. Resumption of specie payments approved in 1875

XV. Election of 1876
    A. Elimination of Grant and Blaine
    B. Republicans nominate Hayes
    C. Democrats nominate Tilden
    D. Views of the parties
    E. Results of the popular vote
    F. The Electoral Commission
    G. Electoral compromise
      1. Promises of each side
      2. Promises filled and unfilled
    H. The end of Reconstruction
      1. A betrayal of the blacks?
      2. An enduring legacy

KEY ITEMS OF CHRONOLOGY

Lincoln's plan for Reconstruction announced	1863
Thirteenth Amendment ratified	1865
Creation of Freedmen's Bureau	1865
Assassination of Lincoln	April 14, 1865
Johnson's plan for Reconstruction announced	May 29, 1865
Veto of Freedmen's Bureau Extension Bill	February 1866
Congress overrode Johnson's veto of Civil Rights Bill	April 1866
Ku Klux Klan organized in the South	1866
Military Reconstruction Act	March 2, 1867
Johnson replaced Stanton with Grant as secretary of war	August 1867
House voted to impeach Johnson	February 1868
Trial of Johnson in Senate	March 5 to May 26, 1868
Fourteenth Amendment ratified	1868
All southern states except Mississippi, Texas, and Virginia readmitted to Congress	June 1868
Texas v. White decision of Supreme Court	1869
Grant administrations	1869–1877
Mississippi, Texas, and Virginia readmitted	1870
Fifteenth Amendment ratified	1870
Resumption Act	1875

TERMS TO MASTER

Listed below are some important terms or people with which you should be familiar after you complete the study of this chapter. Identify each name or term.

1. Freedmen's Bureau
2. Wade-Davis Bill
3. "iron clad oath"
4. black codes
5. Radicals
6. Fourteenth Amendment
7. Military Reconstruction
8. Command of the Army Act
9. Tenure of Office Act
10. carpetbaggers and scalawags
11. Ku Klux Klan
12. Liberal Republicans
13. Jay Gould
14. Crédit-Mobilier
15. Samuel J. Tilden
16. Compromise of 1877

VOCABULARY BUILDING

Listed below are some words used in this chapter. Look in the dictionary for the meaning of each.

1. usurp
2. pernicious
3. intransigence
4. repressive
5. inversion
6. foment
7. boor
8. appellate
9. impeachment
10. rescind
11. jaundiced
12. despotism
13. cesspool
14. buccaneering

EXERCISES FOR UNDERSTANDING

When you have completed reading the chapter, answer each of the following questions. If you have difficulty, go back to the text and reread the section of the chapter related to the question.

Multiple-Choice Questions

Select the letter of the response that best completes the statement.

1. Southerners received the right to form new state governments as soon as 10 percent of a state's 1860 voters had sworn allegiance to the United States, according to the Reconstruction plans proposed by
   A. Lincoln.
   B. Andrew Johnson.
   C. Sen. Benjamin Wade and Rep. Henry Winter Davis.
   D. the Radical Republicans.
2. The Reconstruction policies of the Radical Republicans were probably motivated by
   A. a humanitarian concern for the former slaves.
   B. hopes for Republican power in the South.
   C. bitterness over having to fight the costly war.
   D. all of the above
3. The Fourteenth Amendment to the Constitution
   A. outlawed slavery.
   B. guaranteed citizens the equal protection of the laws.
   C. specifically gave the former slaves the right to vote.
   D. ended Reconstruction in the South.
4. Johnson was impeached for
   A. embezzling federal funds.
   B. refusing to obey the Tenure of Office Act.
   C. refusing to turn documents over to Congress for their investigation.
   D. all of the above.
5. In the southern Reconstruction governments, blacks frequently
   A. served as state governors.
   B. controlled the legislatures.
   C. dominated delegations to the national Congress.
   D. none of the above
6. The Radical southern governments during Reconstruction
   A. were unusually honest and moral.
   B. operated frugally and did not go into debt.
   C. refused to aid private corporations such as railroads.
   D. gave unusual attention to education and poor relief.
7. U. S. Grant was guilty of
   A. refusing to turn documents over to Congress for its investigation.
   B. trying to block the implementation of Reconstruction laws.
   C. choosing his appointees unwisely.
   D. taking funds from the federal treasury.
8. The Compromise of 1877 included provisions for
   A. the impeachment of Grant for corruption.
   B. an end to Radical Reconstruction in the South.
   C. a southerner as Speaker of the House.
   D. all of the above

True-False Questions

Indicate whether each statement is true or false.

1. The problem of Reconstruction began in 1865 with the conclusion of the war.
2. The black codes were laws enacted by southern legislatures that were controlled by the former slaves.
3. Congress generally accepted the "forfeited rights theory" in explaining secession.
4. The Military Reconstruction Act did not provide for a radical reconstruction of the South.
5. Scalawags were white, southern-born Republicans.
6. Andrew Johnson was never elected president.
7. The Crédit-Mobilier was involved in trading greenbacks to France for gold.
8. Grant as president sought to encourage

inflation through the issuing of more greenbacks by the federal government.

Essay Questions

1. Discuss the impact of the Civil War on the South, the North, and the slaves.
2. Compare and contrast the Reconstruction plans of Presidents Lincoln and Johnson.
3. Assess the Radical southern governments and their accomplishments.
4. Radical Reconstruction was not imposed until two years after the end of the Civil War and caused bitter opposition from the whites in the South. Would it have been better accepted if it had been imposed in May 1865 instead of March 1867? Explain why or why not.
5. Why was Andrew Johnson impeached? What was the outcome?
6. What were the major provisions of the Fourteenth Amendment?
7. Explain the provisions of the Compromise of 1877 and its effects on the South.

READINGS

Reading 1. Claude Bowers Sees Venal Radicals Torturing the South

Like other significant periods in American history, the Reconstruction era has gone through cycles of interpretation. Some of the earliest scholarly work on the period was carried out by William A. Dunning and his students, who believed that the Radicals sought to impose their rule on the South for selfish motives of personal gain. Later revisionists have considerably altered that view. The passage below comes from a popular account of Reconstruction written in 1929. It presents the negative image of Radical motives and accomplishments.

If Hilaire Belloc is right in his opinion that "readable history is melodrama," the true story of the twelve tragic years that followed the death of Lincoln should be entertaining. They were years of revolutionary turmoil, with the elemental passions predominant, and with broken bones and bloody noses among the fighting factionalists. The prevailing note was one of tragedy, though, as we shall see, there was an abundance of comedy, and not a little of farce. Never have American public men in responsible positions, directing the destiny of the Nation, been so brutal, hypocritical, and corrupt. The Constitution was treated as a doormat on which politicians and army officers wiped their feet after wading in the muck. Never has the Supreme Court been treated with such ineffable contempt, and never has that tribunal so often cringed before the clamor of the mob.

So appalling is the picture of these revolutionary years that even historians have preferred to overlook many essential things. Thus, Andrew Johnson, who fought the bravest battle for constitutional liberty and for the preservation of our institutions ever waged by an Executive, until recently was left in the pillory to which unscrupulous gamblers for power consigned him, because the unvarnished truth that vindicates him makes so many statues in public squares and parks seem a bit grotesque. That Johnson was maligned by his enemies because he was seeking honestly to carry out the conciliatory and wise policy of Lincoln is now generally understood, but even now few realize how intensely Lincoln was hated by the Radicals at the time of his death.

A complete understanding of this period calls for a reappraisal of many public men. Some statesmen we have been taught to reverence will appear in these pages in sorry rôles. Others, who played conspicuous parts, but have been denied the historical recognition due them, are introduced and shown in action. Thus the able leaders of the minority in Congress are given fuller treatment than has been fashionable, since they represented more Americans, North and South, than the leaders of the Radical majority, and were nearer right on the issues of reconstruction. Thus, too, the brilliant and colorful leaders and spokesmen of the South are given their proper place in the dramatic struggle for the preservation of Southern civilization and the redemption of their people. I have sought to re-create the black and bloody drama of these years, to show the leaders of the fighting factions at close range, to picture the moving masses, both whites and blacks, in North and South, surging crazily under the influence of the poisonous propaganda on which they were fed.

That the Southern people literally were put to the torture is vaguely understood, but even historians have shrunk from the unhappy task of showing us the torture chambers. It is impossible to grasp the real significance of the revolutionary proceedings of the rugged conspirators working out the policies of Thaddeus Stevens without making many journeys among the Southern people, and seeing with our own eyes the indignities to which they were subjected. Through many unpublished contemporary family letters and diaries, I have tried to show the psychological effect upon them of the despotic policies of which they were the victims. Brutal men, inspired by personal ambition or party motives, assumed the pose of philanthropists and patriots, and thus deceived and misguided vast numbers of well-meaning people in the North.

[From Claude G. Bowers, *The Tragic Era: The Revolution after Lincoln* (New York: Blue Ribbon Books, 1929), pp. v–vi]

Reading 2. William A. Dunning Explains the Failure of Reconstruction

William A. Dunning, a historian at Columbia University around the turn of the century, wrote a synthesis of Reconstruction from a southern point of view and directed a school of scholars who investigated developments in states in the South from a similar viewpoint. In these excerpts Dunning, while explaining the failure of Reconstruction, reveals his attitude about the corruption and inadequacy of Reconstruction governments and his reservations about race. What insights do you find in his views?

The leading motive of the reconstruction had been, at the inception of the process, to insure to the freedmen an effective protection of their civil rights,—of life, liberty, and property. In the course of the process, the chief stress came to be laid on the endowment of the blacks with full political rights,—with the electoral franchise and eligibility to office. And by the time the process was complete, a very important, if not the most important part had been played by the desire and the purpose to secure to the Republican party the permanent control of several Southern states in which hitherto such a political organization had been unknown. This last motive had a plausible and widely accepted justification in the view that the rights of the negro and the "results of the war" in general would be secure only if the national government should remain indefinitely in Republican hands, and that therefore the strengthening of the party was a primary dictate of patriotism.

Through the operation of these various motives successive and simultaneous, the completion of the reconstruction showed the following situation: (1) the negroes were in the enjoyment of the equal political rights with the whites; (2) the Republican party was in vigorous life in all the Southern states, and in firm control of many of them; and (3) the negroes exercised an influence in political affairs out of all relation to their intelligence or property, and, since so many of the whites were defranchised, excessive even in proportion to their numbers. At the present day, in the same states, the negroes enjoy practically no political rights; the Republican party is but the shadow of a name; and the influence of the negroes in political affairs is nil. This contrast suggests what has been involved in the undoing of reconstruction.

Before the last state was restored to the Union the process was well under way through which the resumption of control by the whites was to be effected. The tendency in this direction was greatly promoted by conditions within the Republican party itself. Two years of supremacy in those states which had been restored in 1868 had revealed unmistakable evidences of moral and political weakness in the governments. The personnel of the party was declining in character through the return to the North of the more substantial of the carpet-baggers, who found Southern conditions, both social and industrial, far from what they had anticipated, and through the very frequent instances in which the "scalawags" ran to open disgrace. Along with this deterioration in the white element of the party, the negroes who rose to prominence and leadership were very frequently of a type which acquired and practiced the tricks and knavery rather than the useful arts of politics, and the vicious courses of these negroes strongly confirmed the prejudices of the whites. But at the same time that the incapacity of the party in power to administer any government was becoming demonstrable the problems with which it was required to cope were made by its adversaries such as would have taxed the capacity of the most efficient statesmen the world could produce. . . . No attention was paid to the claim that the manifest inefficiency and viciousness of the Republican governments afforded a partial, if not wholly adequate explanation of their overthrow. Not even the relative quiet and order that followed the triumph of the whites in these states were recognized as justifying the new regime.

[From William A. Dunning, "The Undoing of Reconstruction," in *The Atlantic Monthly*, October 1901, pp. 437–438]

Reading 3. Eric Foner Contends That Reconstruction Did Not Go Far Enough

Historical scholarship on the Reconstruction era continues to grow at a remarkable rate. In the following excerpt Eric Foner summarizes some of the most recent scholarship and suggests a new way to view Reconstruction.

Despite the excellence of recent writing and the continual expansion of our knowledge of the period, historians of Reconstruction today face a unique dilemma. An old interpretation has been overthrown, but a coherent new synthesis has yet to take its place. The revisionists of the 1960s effectively established a series of negative points: the Reconstruction governments were not as bad as had been portrayed, black supremacy was a myth, the Radicals were not cynical manipulators of the freedmen. Yet no convincing overall portrait of the quality of political and social life emerged from their writings.

. . . a new portrait of Reconstruction ought to begin by viewing it not as a specific time period, bounded by the years 1865 and 1877, but as an episode in a prolonged historical process—American society's adjustment to the consequences of the Civil War and emancipation.

. . . the focal point of Reconstruction was the social revolution known as emancipation. Plantation slavery was simultaneously a system of labor, a form of racial domination, and the foundation upon which arose a distinctive ruling class within the South. Its demise threw open the most fundamental questions of economy, society, and politics. A new system of labor, social, racial, and political relations had to be created to replace slavery.

Few modern scholars believe the Reconstruction governments established in the South in 1867 and 1868 fulfilled the aspirations of their humble constituents. While their achievements in such realms as education, civil rights, and the economic rebuilding of the South are now widely appreciated, historians today believe they failed to affect either the economic plight of the emancipated slave or the ongoing transformation of independent white farmers into cotton tenants. Yet their opponents did perceive the Reconstruction governments in precisely this way—as representatives of a revolution that had put the bottom rail, both racial and economic, on top. This perception helps explain the ferocity of the attacks leveled against them and the pervasiveness of violence in the postemancipation South.

The spectacle of black men voting and holding office was anathema to large numbers of Southern whites. Even more disturbing, at least in the view of those who still controlled the plantation regions of the South, was the emergence of local officials, black and white, who sympathized with the plight of the black laborer. . . . During presidential Reconstruction, and after "Redemption," with planters and their allies in control of politics, the law emerged as a means of stabilizing and promoting the plantation system. If Radical Reconstruction failed to redistribute the land of the South, the ouster of the planter class from control of politics at least ensured that the sanctions of the criminal law would not be employed to discipline the black labor force.

An understanding of this fundamental conflict over the relation between government and society helps explain the pervasive complaints concerning corruption and "extravagance" during Radical Reconstruction. Corruption there was aplenty; tax rates did rise sharply. More significant than the rate of taxation, however, was the change in its incidence. For the first time, planters and white farmers had to pay a significant portion of their income to the government, while propertyless blacks often escaped scot-free. Several states, moreover, enacted heavy taxes on uncultivated land to discourage land speculation and force land onto the market, benefiting, it was hoped, the freedmen.

As time passed, complaints about the "extravagance" and corruption of Southern governments found a sympathetic audience among influential Northerners. The Democratic charge that universal suffrage in the South was responsible for high taxes and governmental extravagance coincided with a rising conviction among the urban middle classes of the North that city government had to be taken out of the hands of the immigrant poor and returned to the "best men"—the educated, professional, financially independent citizens unable to exert much political influence at a time of mass parties and machine politics. Increasingly the "respectable" middle classes began to retreat from the very notion of universal suffrage. The poor were no longer perceived as honest producers, the backbone of the social order; now they became the "dangerous classes," the "mob." As the historian Francis Parkman put it, too much power rested with "masses of imported ignorance and hereditary ineptitude." To Parkman the Irish of the Northern cities and the blacks of the South were equally incapable of utilizing the ballot: "Witness the municipal corruptions of New York, and the monstrosities of negro rule in South Carolina." Such attitudes helped to justify Northern inaction as, one by one, the Reconstruction regimes of the South were overthrown by political violence.

In the end, then, neither the abolition of slavery nor Reconstruction succeeded in resolving the debate over the meaning of freedom in American life. Twenty years before the American Civil War, writing about the prospect of abolition in France's colonies, Alexis de Tocqueville had written, "If the Negroes have the right to become free, the [planters] have the incontestable right not to be ruined by the Negroes' freedom." And in the United States, as in nearly every plantation society that experienced the end of slavery, a rigid social and political dichotomy between former master and former slave, an ideology of racism, and a dependent labor force with limited economic opportunities all survived abolition. Unless one means by freedom the simple fact of not being a slave, emancipation thrust blacks into a kind of no-man's land, a partial freedom that made a mockery of the American ideal of equal citizenship.

Yet by the same token the ultimate outcome underscores the uniqueness of Reconstruction itself. Alone among the societies that abolished slavery in the nineteenth century, the United States, for a moment, offered the freedmen a measure of political control over their own destinies. However brief its sway, Reconstruction allowed scope for a remarkable political and social mobilization of the black community. It opened doors of opportunity that could never be completely closed. Reconstruction transformed the lives of Southern blacks in ways unmeasurable by statistics and unreachable by law. It raised their expectations and aspirations, redefined their status in relation to the larger society, and allowed space for the creation of institutions that enabled them to survive the repression that followed. And it established constitutional principles of civil and political equality that, while flagrantly violated after Redemption, planted the seeds of future struggle.

[From Eric Foner, "The New View of Reconstruction," in *American Heritage* 34, no. 6 (October-November 1983): 13–15]

Questions for Reflection

What evidence is there in the first two readings to show that Dunning found Reconstruction less despicable a development than Bowers did? What good does Dunning seem to imply came from Reconstruction? Select some of the words and phrases which Bowers used to give an emotional tone to his account. Is Dunning more convincing to the reader? What appear to be Dunning's views on race?

What does Dunning mean by "The failure of Radicalism is thus a part of the wider failure of bourgeois liberalism to solve the problems of the new age which was dawning"?

According to Eric Foner, how did Reconstruction lead to the ouster of the planter class from control of politics and why was that important? How did attitudes toward blacks in Reconstruction interact with attitudes toward immigrants and other oppressed groups in the North? Why does Foner think that Reconstruction did not succeed in giving blacks freedom?

All three passages find a failure in Reconstruction from one perspective or another. How do you think the problems of Reconstruction of the South could have been better solved?

ANSWERS TO MULTIPLE-CHOICE AND TRUE-FALSE QUESTIONS

Multiple-Choice Questions

1-A, 2-D, 3-B, 4-B, 5-D, 6-D, 7-C, 8-B

True-False Questions

1-F, 2-F, 3-T, 4-T, 5-T, 6-T, 7-F, 8-F

18

NEW FRONTIERS: SOUTH AND WEST

CHAPTER OBJECTIVES

After you complete the reading and study of this chapter you should be able to

1. Explain the concept of the New South, its development, and how it affected the South after the Civil War.
2. Account for the rise of the Bourbons to power in the South and explain their impact on the region.
3. Explain the causes and process of disfranchisement of blacks in the South.
4. Compare the views of Washington and Du Bois on the place of blacks in American life.
5. Describe the Indian wars and explain the new Indian policy of 1887.
6. Describe the rise and decline of the cattle industry.
7. Describe the problems of farming on the western frontier.
8. Explain the importance of Turner's theory of the significance of the frontier in American history.

CHAPTER OUTLINE

I. The New South
  A. Concept of the New South
    1. Henry Grady's background
    2. His vision
    3. Other prophets of the New South creed
  B. Economic growth
    1. Growth of cotton textile manufacturing
    2. Development of the tobacco industry
      a. Duke family
      b. Techniques used by Buck Duke for growth
      c. Creation and breakup of the American Tobacco Company
    3. Coal production
    4. Lumbering
    5. Beginnings of petroleum and hydroelectric power
  C. Agriculture in the New South
    1. Limited diversity in agriculture
    2. Features of sharecropping and tenancy
    3. Impact of the crop lien system
  D. Role of the Bourbon Redeemers
    1. Nature of the Bourbons
    2. Bourbon economic policies
      a. Laissez-faire
      b. Retrenchment in government spending
      c. Assistance of private philanthropy
      d. Convict lease system
      e. Repudiation of Confederate debts in some states
      f. Positive contributions of the Bourbons

g. Varied development of color lines in social relations

E. Disfranchisement of blacks
1. Impetus for elimination of the black vote
   a. Fears of retrogression
   b. Impact of Populists
2. Techniques used to exclude blacks
   a. Mississippi
   b. Louisiana
3. Spread of segregation
   a. Segregation in railway cars
   b. Impact of *Civil Rights Cases,* 1883
   c. Impact of *Plessy v. Ferguson,* 1896
4. Spread of violence against blacks

F. Clash of Booker T. Washington and W. E. B. Du Bois

II. The New West
A. Nature of the West and its settlement after the war
B. Developments that altered the Great American Desert
C. The mining frontier
1. Pattern of mining development
2. Locations of major mineral discoveries
3. Development of new states
D. Displacement of the Indians
1. Conflicts that arose during the Civil War
2. Establishment of Indian Peace Commission, 1867

a. Policy of large reservations
b. Agreements with the Indians in 1867 and 1868
3. Continued resistance of Indians
   a. Massacre at Little Big Horn
   b. Conquest of Sioux and others
   c. Significance of Chief Joseph and Nez Perce
4. Impact of annihilation of buffalo herds
5. Stirrings for reform in Indian policy
   a. Eastern view of Indian slaughter
   b. Role of Helen Hunt Jackson
6. Dawes Severalty Act, 1887
   a. Concept of new policy
   b. Provisions of Dawes and subsequent acts
   c. Impact of new policy

E. The cattle industry in the West
1. Development of the open range
2. Long drives after the Civil War
   a. Joseph McCoy
   b. Features of the cowtown
3. Codes of the open range

F. The farming frontier
1. Land policy after the Civil War
2. Changed institutions in the West
3. Efforts for reclamation of arid lands
4. An assessment of land distribution
5. Aspects of farming and life on the Great Plains

G. Turner's frontier thesis
1. Turner's claims for the frontier
2. Other views

KEY ITEMS OF CHRONOLOGY

Homestead Act	1862
First of the long drives	1866
Indian Peace Commission settlements	1867–1868
Civil Rights Cases	1883
Dawes Severalty Act	1887
Mississippi Constitution incorporates disfranchisement of blacks	1890
Census shows frontier closed	1890
Turner frontier thesis presented	1893
B. T. Washington's "Atlanta Compromise" speech	1895
Plessy v. Ferguson	1896
Disfranchisement of blacks essentially completed in southern states	1910

TERMS TO MASTER

Listed below are some important terms or people with which you should be familiar after you complete the study of this chapter. Explain the significance of each name or term.

1. Henry W. Grady
2. James Buchanan Duke
3. sharecropping
4. crop lien system
5. Bourbons
6. Convict lease system
7. Mississippi Plan for disfranchisement
8. grandfather clauses
9. segregation
10. *Plessy v. Ferguson*
11. Booker T. Washington
12. W. E. B. Du Bois
13. Great American Desert
14. Indian Peace Commission
15. George A. Custer
16. Chief Joseph
17. *A Century of Dishonor*
18. Dawes Severalty Act
19. "dry farming"
20. Frederick Jackson Turner

VOCABULARY BUILDING

Listed below are some words used in this chapter. Look up each word in your dictionary.

1. lien
2. epithet
3. austerity
4. scrimping
5. paragons
6. disfranchise
7. bestiality
8. octoroon
9. salved
10. inexorable
11. spoliation
12. bushwhackers
13. sedentary
14. sodbusters

EXERCISES FOR UNDERSTANDING

When you have completed reading the chapter, answer each of the following questions. If you have difficulty, go back and reread the section of the chapter related to the question.

Multiple-Choice Questions

Select the letter of the response that best completes the statement.

1. James B. Duke's greatest contribution to the South's progress was in
   A. development of the cigarette industry.
   B. promotion of education.
   C. inventions for textile manufacturing.
   D. stimulating competition among industries in the South.

2. The most significant impact of the crop lien system in the South was that it
   A. made possible cash payments for goods.
   B. provided a source of labor in the post-Reconstruction South.
   C. made possible low-interest-rate loans for blacks.
   D. encouraged the South to raise only one crop, cotton.

3. Mississippi's techniques for disfranchising blacks included all of the following *except* a
   A. residency requirement.
   B. poll tax.
   C. grandfather clause.
   D. literacy test.

4. "In all things that are purely social we can be as separate as the five fingers, yet one as the hand in all things essential to mutual progress," said
   A. Henry Grady.
   B. W. E. B. Du Bois.
   C. the Supreme Court in *Plessy v. Ferguson*.
   D. Booker T. Washington.

5. The idea of the West as the Great American Desert was overcome by
   A. the rush for gold and silver.
   B. the transcontinental railroad.

C. the rise of cattle ranching.
D. all of the above

6. In the Battle of Little Big Horn, General George A. Custer fought
   A. gold and silver miners in Colorado.
   B. Indians in the Montana territory.
   C. "Calamity Jane" and "Wild Bill Hickok" in South Dakota.
   D. Indians in the Southwest.

7. Helen Hunt Jackson's *A Century of Dishonor* aroused concern about the
   A. plight of Indians.
   B. need for law and order in western mining towns.
   C. disfranchisement of southern blacks.
   D. corruption in the Grant administration.

8. The institutions of the West were shaped most by
   A. government land policies.
   B. climate.
   C. barbed wire.
   D. cattle.

True-False Questions

Indicate whether each statement is true or false.

1. Henry Grady's view of the New South emphasized the development of industry.
2. The Bourbons increased spending for public education in the South.
3. In the 1870s Bourbons quickly ended all black influence in southern politics.

4. The *Plessy v. Ferguson* decision included a ruling that states could not interfere with the rights of blacks.
5. A leading critic of Booker T. Washington was W. E. B. Du Bois.
6. General George Custer was defeated at the battle of Little Big Horn.
7. The decline of buffalo herds played a significant role in ending Indian resistance in the West.
8. Between 1851 and 1871 the federal government granted railroads about 200 million acres in the West.

Essay Questions

1. Describe the economic growth in the South after Reconstruction.
2. Describe three techniques used to disfranchise blacks in the South.
3. Explain how the sharecropping and tenant systems worked in southern agriculture.
4. Contrast the visions of Booker T. Washington and W. E. B. Du Bois for freed blacks.
5. What impact did the boom and bust in cattle ranching have on the settlement of the West?
6. Did the federal government's Indian policy have more or less effect on the development of the West than its land policy?
7. How did black social and political life change in the South during the 1890s?

DOCUMENTS

Document 1. Booker T. Washington Proposes the "Atlanta Compromise"

Invited to appear before a national audience at the Atlanta Exposition in 1895, Booker T. Washington carefully honed a speech asserting the importance of the black contribution to America and the South, but avoiding the offending of white sensibilities. The speech was widely acclaimed among whites and blacks alike.

One-third of the population of the South is of the Negro race. No enterprise seeking the material, civil, or moral welfare of this section can disregard this element of our population and reach the highest success. . . .

Ignorant and inexperienced, it is not strange that in the first years of our new life we began at the top instead of at the bottom; that a seat in Congress or the state legislature was more sought than real estate or industrial skill; that the political convention or stump speaking had more attractions than starting a dairy farm or truck garden.

A ship lost at sea for many days suddenly sighted a friendly vessel. From the mast of the unfortunate vessel was seen a signal, "Water, water; we die of thirst!" The answer from the friendly vessel at once came back, "Cast down your bucket where you are." A second time the signal, "Water, water; send us water!" ran up from the distressed vessel, and was answered, "Cast down your bucket where you are." The captain of the distressed vessel, at last heeding the injunction, cast down his bucket, and it came up full of fresh, sparkling water from the mouth of the Amazon River. To those of my race who depend on bettering their condition in a foreign land or who underestimate the importance of cultivating friendly relations with the Southern white man, who is their next-door neighbour, I would say: "Cast down your bucket where you are"—cast it down in making friends in every manly way of the people of all races by whom we are surrounded.

Cast it down in agriculture, mechanics, in commerce, in domestic service, and in the professions. And in this connection it is well to bear in mind that whatever other sins the South may be called to bear, when it comes to business, pure and simple, it is in the South that the Negro is given a man's chance in the commercial world, and in nothing is this Exposition more eloquent than in emphasizing this chance. Our greatest danger is that in the great leap from slavery to freedom we may overlook the fact that the masses of us are to live by the productions of our hands, and fail to keep in mind that we shall prosper in proportion as we learn to dignify and glorify common labour and put brains and skill into the common occupation of life; shall prosper in proportion as we learn to draw the line between the superficial and the substantial, the ornamental gewgaws of life and the useful. No race can prosper till it learns that there is as much dignity in tilling a field as in writing a poem. It is at the bottom of life we must begin, and not at the top. Nor should we permit our grievances to overshadow our opportunities.

To those of the white race who look to the incoming of those of foreign birth and strange tongue and habits for the prosperity of the South, were I permitted I would repeat what I say to my own race, "Cast down your bucket where you are." Cast it down among the eight millions of Negroes whose habits you know, whose fidelity and love you have tested in days when to have proved treacherous meant the ruin of your firesides. Cast down your bucket among these people who have, without strikes and labour wars, tilled your fields, cleared your forests, builded your railroads and cities, and brought forth treasures from the bowels of the earth, and helped make possible this magnificent representation of the progress of the

South. Casting down your bucket among my people, helping and encouraging them as you are doing on these grounds, and to education of head, hand, and heart, you will find that they will buy your surplus land, make blossom the waste places in your fields, and run your factories. While doing this, you can be sure in the future, as in the past, that you and your families will be surrounded by the most patient, faithful, law-abiding, and unresentful people that the world has seen. As we have proved our loyalty to you in the past, in nursing your children, watching by the sick-bed of your mothers and fathers, and often following them with tear-dimmed eyes to their graves, so in the future, in our humble way, we shall stand by you with a devotion that no foreigner can approach, ready to lay down our lives, if need be, in defence of yours, interlacing our industrial, commercial, civil, and religious life with yours in a way that shall make the interests of both races one. In all things that are purely social we can be as separate as the fingers, yet one as the hand in all things essential to mutual progress.

There is no defence or security for any of us except in the highest intelligence and development of all. If anywhere there are efforts tending to curtail the fullest growth of the Negro, let these efforts be turned into stimulating, encouraging, and making him the most useful and intelligent citizen. Effort or means so invested will pay a thousand per cent interest. These efforts will be twice blessed— "blessing him that gives and him that takes."

The wisest among my race understand that the agitation of questions of social equality is the extremest folly, and that progress in the enjoyment of all the privileges that will come to us must be the result of severe and constant struggle rather than of artificial forcing. No race that has anything to contribute to the markets of the world is long in any degree ostracized. It is important and right that all privileges of the law be ours, but it is vastly more important that we be prepared for the exercises of these privileges. The opportunity to earn a dollar in a factory just now is worth infinitely more than the opportunity to spend a dollar in an opera-house.

[Booker T. Washington, *Up from Slavery* (New York: Doubleday, Page & Co., 1902), pp. 218–224]

Document 2. W. E. B. Du Bois Disagrees with Washington

Educated at Fisk and Harvard Universities, W. E. B. Du Bois became the leader of blacks who disagreed with Washington's prescriptions. The passage below reflects Du Bois's disagreements with Washington.

Mr. Washington represents in Negro thought the old attitude of adjustment and submission; but adjustment at such a peculiar time as to make his programme unique. This is an age of unusual economic development, and Mr. Washington's programme naturally takes an economic cast, becoming a gospel of Work and Money to such an extent as apparently almost completely to overshadow the higher aims of life. Moreover, this is an age when the more advanced races are coming in closer contact with the less developed races, and the race-feeling is therefore intensified; and Mr. Washington's programme practically accepts the alleged inferiority of the Negro races. Again, in our own land, the reaction from the sentiment of war time has given impetus to race-prejudice against Negroes, and Mr. Washington withdraws many of the high demands of Negroes as men and American citizens. In other periods of intensified prejudice all the Negro's tendency to self-assertion has been called forth; at this period a policy of submission is advocated. In the history of nearly all other races and peoples the doctrine preached at such crises has been that manly self-respect is worth more than lands and houses, and that a people who voluntarily surrender such respect, or cease striving for it, are not worth civilizing.

In answer to this, it has been claimed that the Negro can survive only through submission. Mr. Washington distinctly asks that black people give up, at least for the present, three things—

First, political power,

Second, insistence on civil rights,

Third, higher education of Negro youth,—and concentrate all their energies on industrial education, the accumulation of wealth, and the conciliation of the South. This policy has been courageously and insistently advocated for over fifteen years, and has been triumphant for perhaps ten years. As a result of this tender of the palm-branch, what has been the return? In these years there have occurred:

1. The disfranchisement of the Negro.

2. The legal creation of a distinct status of civil inferiority for the Negro.

3. The steady withdrawal of aid from institutions for the higher training of the Negro.

These movements are not, to be sure, direct results of Mr. Washington's teachings; but this propaganda has, without a shadow of doubt, helped their speedier accomplishment. The question then comes: Is it possible, and probable, that nine millions of men can make effective progress in economic lines if they are deprived of political rights, made a servile caste, and allowed only the most meagre chance for developing their exceptional men? If history and reason give any distinct answer to these questions, it is an emphatic *No*. And Mr. Washington thus faces the triple paradox of his career:

1. He is striving nobly to make Negro artisans, businessmen and property-owners; but it is utterly impossible, under modern competitive methods, for workingmen and property-owners to defend their rights and exist without the right of suffrage.

2. He insists on thrift and self-respect, but at the same time counsels a silent submission to civic inferiority such as is bound to sap the manhood of any race in the long run.

3. He advocates common-school and industrial training, and depreciates institutions of higher learning; but neither the Negro common-schools, nor Tuskegee itself, could remain open a day were it not for teachers trained in Negro colleges, or trained by their graduates.

This triple paradox in Mr. Washington's position is the object of criticism by two classes of colored Americans. One class is spiritually descended from Toussaint the Savior, through Gabriel, Vesey, and

Turner, and they represent the attitude of revolt and revenge; they hate the white South blindly and distrust the white race generally, and so far as they agree on definite action, think that the Negro's only hope lies in emigration beyond the borders of the United States. And yet, by the irony of fate, nothing has more effectually made this programme seem hopeless than the recent course of the United States toward weaker and darker peoples in the West Indies, Hawaii, and the Philippines,—for where in the world may we go and be safe from lying and brute force?

The other class of Negroes who cannot agree with Mr. Washington has hitherto said little aloud. They deprecate the sight of scattered counsels, or internal disagreement; and especially they dislike making their just criticism of a useful and earnest man an excuse for a general discharge of venom from small-minded opponents. . . . Such men feel in conscience bound to ask of this nation three things:

1. The right to vote.
2. Civic equality.
3. The education of youth according to ability.

They acknowledge Mr. Washington's invaluable service in counselling patience and courtesy in such demands; they do not ask that ignorant black men vote when ignorant whites are debarred, or that any reasonable restrictions in the suffrage should not be applied; they know that the low social level of the mass of the race is responsible for much discrimination against it, but they also know, and the nation knows, that relentless color-prejudice is more often a cause than a result of the Negro's degradation; they seek the abatement of this relic of barbarism, and not its systematic encouragement and pampering by all agencies of social power from the Associated Press to the Church of Christ. They advocate, with Mr. Washington, a broad system of Negro common schools supplemented by thorough industrial training; but they are surprised that a man of Mr. Washington's insight cannot see that no such educational system ever has rested or can rest on any other basis than that of the well-equipped college and university, and they insist that there is a demand for a few such institutions throughout the South to train the best of the Negro youth as teachers, professional men, and leaders.

This group of men honor Mr. Washington for his attitude of conciliation toward the white South; they accept the "Atlanta Compromise" in its broadest interpretation; they recognize, with him, many signs of promise, many men of high purpose and fair judgment, in this section; they know that no easy task has been laid upon a region already tottering under heavy burdens. But, nevertheless, they insist that the way to truth and right lies in straightforward honesty, not in indiscriminate flattery; in praising those of the South who do well and criticising uncompromisingly those who do ill; in taking advantage of the opportunities at hand and urging their fellows to do the same, but at the same time in remembering that only a firm adherence to their higher ideals and aspirations will ever keep those ideals within the realm of possibility. They do not expect that the free right to vote, to enjoy civic rights, and to be educated, will come in a moment; they do not expect to see the bias and prejudices of years disappear at the blast of a trumpet; but they are absolutely certain that the way for a people to gain their reasonable rights is not by voluntarily throwing them away and insisting that they do not want them; that the way for a people to gain respect is not by continually belittling and ridiculing themselves; that, on the contrary, Negroes must insist continually, in season and out of season, that voting is necessary to modern manhood, that color discrimination is barbarism, and that black boys need education as well as white boys.

[W. E. B. Du Bois, "Of Mr. Booker T. Washington and Others," in *Souls of Black Folk* (Chicago: A. C. McClurg, 1903), pp. 50–55]

Questions for Reflection

What evidence do you see in Washington's speech that he was trying not to offend his predominantly white audience? Do you see evidence that Washington feared that blacks might be replaced by another group? What groups? How justified was his fear?

Does Du Bois seem to acknowledge the tightrope which Washington had to walk in developing his compromise position?

Are Du Bois's criticisms of Washington's position valid? Which of these men had a better concept of what blacks needed to do? Why?

ANSWERS TO MULTIPLE-CHOICE AND TRUE-FALSE QUESTIONS

Multiple-Choice Questions

1-A, 2-D, 3-C, 4-D, 5-D, 6-B, 7-A, 8-B

True-False Questions

1-T, 2-F, 3-F, 4-F, 5-T, 6-T, 7-T, 8-T

19

BIG BUSINESS AND ORGANIZED LABOR

CHAPTER OBJECTIVES

After you complete the reading and study of this chapter you should be able to:

1. Describe the economic impact of the Civil War.
2. Explain the important factors in the growth of the economy in the late nineteenth century.
3. Describe the role of the major entrepreneurs like Rockefeller, Carnegie, and Morgan.
4. Account for the limited growth of unions in this period, and the success of the Knights of Labor and the American Federation of Labor.
5. Describe the major labor confrontations in the period.
6. Account for the limited appeal of socialism for American labor.

CHAPTER OUTLINE

I. The post–Civil War economy
   A. Economic changes in the 1869–1899 period
   B. Railroad building
      1. The transcontinental plan
         a. Central Pacific
            1. organizers
            2. Chinese laborers
         b. Union Pacific
      2. Financing the railroads
         a. Crédit-Mobilier fraud
         b. Jay Gould's work
         c. Cornelius Vanderbilt
      3. Railroads controlled by seven major groups
   C. New products and inventions
      1. Number of patents
      2. Improvements and inventions
      3. Development of the telephone
      4. Edison's work with electricity
   D. Entrepreneurs of the era
      1. Rockefeller and the oil industry
         a. Background
         b. Concentration on refining and transportation
         c. Development of the trust
         d. Evolution of the holding company
      2. Andrew Carnegie and the Gospel of Wealth
         a. Background
         b. Concentration on steel
         c. Philosophy for big business
         d. Other proponents of the Gospel of Wealth
      3. J. P. Morgan and investment banking
         a. Background
         b. Concentration on railroad financing

  c. Control of organizations
  d. Consolidation of the steel
     industry
E. Impact of growth on the distribution of
   wealth
II. Developments in labor
  A. Circumstances for workers
    1. Wages and hours
    2. Living and working conditions
    3. Control by impersonal forces
  B. Obstacles to unions
  C. Molly Maguires
  D. Railroad strike of 1877
    1. Causes
    2. Scope and violence
    3. Effects
  E. Efforts at union building
    1. National Labor Union
    2. Knights of Labor
      a. Early development
      b. Emphasis on the union
      c. Role of Terence Powderly
      d. Victories of the Knights

  e. Haymarket Affair
  f. Lasting influence of the Knights
     of Labor
    3. Development of the American
       Federation of Labor
      a. Development of craft unions
      b. Role of Samuel Gompers
      c. Growth of the union
  F. Violence in the 1890s
    1. Homestead Strike, 1892
    2. Pullman Strike, 1894
      a. Causes
      b. Role of the government
      c. Impact on Eugene V. Debs
  G. Socialism and American labor
    1. Daniel De Leon and Eugene Debs
    2. Social Democratic party
      a. Early work
      b. Height of influence
  H. Rise of the IWW
    1. Sources of strength
    2. Revolutionary goals
    3. Causes for decline

KEY ITEMS OF CHRONOLOGY

National Labor Union formed	1866
Completion of the first transcontinental railroad	1869
Standard Oil of Ohio incorporated	1870
Telephone patented	1876
Incandescent light bulb invented	1879
Terence Powderly became president of the Knights of Labor	1879
First electric current supplied to 85 customers in New York City	1882
Creation of the Standard Oil Trust	1882
Haymarket Affair	1886
Founding of the American Federation of Labor	1886
Pullman Strike	1894
U.S. Steel Corporation formed	1901
IWW founded	1905

TERMS TO MASTER

Listed below are some important terms or people with which you should be familiar after you complete the study of this chapter. Explain the significance of each name or term.

1. Union Pacific
2. transcontinental railroads
3. Crédit-Mobilier
4. Cornelius Vanderbilt
5. Alexander Graham Bell
6. Thomas Alva Edison
7. George Westinghouse
8. John D. Rockefeller
9. Gospel of Wealth
10. Horatio Alger
11. J. Pierpont Morgan
12. United States Steel Company
13. holding company
14. Molly Maguires
15. industrial and craft unions
16. Knights of Labor
17. American Federation of Labor
18. Haymarket Affair
19. Samuel Gompers
20. Pullman Strike
21. Eugene V. Debs
22. Wobblies

VOCABULARY BUILDING

Listed below are some words used in this chapter. Look up each word in your dictionary.

1. cornucopia
2. baron
3. patent
4. prototype
5. trust
6. precarious
7. impromptu
8. jurisdictional
9. idyllic
10. injunction
11. doctrinaire
12. nomadic
13. socialism

EXERCISES FOR UNDERSTANDING

When you have completed reading the chapter, answer each of the following questions. If you have difficulty, go back and reread the section of the chapter related to the question.

Multiple-Choice Questions

Select the letter of the response that best completes the statement.

1. The first transcontinental railroad was built by
   A. the federal government.
   B. private companies granted a monopoly by the government.
   C. private companies with no federal assistance.
   D. private companies with government subsidies.

2. The profiteering of railroad companies included
   A. bribes to congressmen.
   B. construction companies that overcharged for building railroads and made a profit.
   C. shoddy workmanship in building the railroad lines.
   D. all of the above

3. Rockefeller's success depended in large part on
   A. vertical integration.
   B. his ownership of most Pennsylvania oilfields.
   C. corruption of government officials.
   D. many favorable loans from bankers.

4. Andrew Carnegie's Gospel of Wealth called on the rich to
   A. support overseas missionaries.
   B. get richer.
   C. provide for the public good.
   D. help others gain wealth by turning their businesses over to the workers.

5. The social costs of industrialization included
   A. closer relationships between workers and factory owners.
   B. numerous job-related injuries and deaths.

C. rising wages for workers.
D. healthier working conditions for most workers.

6. The Knights of Labor
   A. organized only skilled workers.
   B. shunned politics and strikes.
   C. was damaged by the Haymarket Affair.
   D. all of the above

7. American workers tended to reject unions because
   A. they believed they would only be workers for a short time until they could own their own farms or move up otherwise.
   B. they were so strongly committed to a system of equality and uniform wages for all.
   C. they did not like the association with immigrants in unions.
   D. they thought all unions were corrupt.

8. The leader of the socialist movement in the United States was
   A. Samuel Gompers.
   B. Terence V. Powderly.
   C. Henry Clay Frick.
   D. Eugene V. Debs.

True-False Questions

Indicate whether each statement is true or false.

1. The first big business with large-scale bureaucracies was in the steel industry.
2. The Central Pacific railroad employed many Chinese on its construction crews.

3. George Westinghouse developed air brakes for railroads and alternating electric current.
4. Horatio Alger's novels portrayed the lives of robber barons in the late nineteenth century.
5. In 1900 the average worker in manufacturing worked only about 45 hours per week.
6. The first major interstate strike was led by the Molly Maguires in the coal industry.
7. The American Federation of Labor was an organization of national craft unions.
8. The most conservative labor organization was the Industrial Workers of the World.

Essay Questions

1. List and explain the factors that promoted the growth of industry in the United States in the late nineteenth century.
2. What was the relationship among inventors, entrepreneurs, and great wealth in the late–nineteenth-century United States? Give several examples.
3. Compare and contrast the business practices of J. P. Morgan and Jay Gould.
4. Describe some of the benefits and drawbacks of industrialization for workers. What was their response to it?
5. Explain the appeal of socialism and other forms of radicalism to some American workers.

DOCUMENTS

Document 1. Andrew Carnegie Provides Rules for Disposing of Wealth

As the textbook indicates, Andrew Carnegie developed the concept of the Gospel of Wealth in an essay originally entitled "Wealth." Excerpted below are sections dealing with the best method for a person to use in disposing of his fortune.

It will be understood that *fortunes* are here spoken of, not moderate sums saved by many years of effort, the returns from which are required for the comfortable maintenance and education of families. This is not *wealth*, but only *competence*, which it should be the aim of all to acquire.

There are but three modes in which surplus wealth can be disposed of. It can be left to the families of the decedents; or it can be bequeathed for public purposes; or, finally, it can be administered during their lives by its possessors. Under the first and second modes most of the wealth of the world that has reached the few has hitherto been applied. Let us in turn consider each of these modes. The first is the most injudicious. In monarchical countries, the estates and the greatest portion of the wealth are left to the first son, that the vanity of the parent may be gratified by the thought that his name and title are to descend to succeeding generations unimpaired. The condition of this class in Europe to-day teaches the futility of such hopes or ambitions. The successors have become impoverished through their follies or from the fall in the value of land. . . . Under republican institutions the division of property among the children is much fairer, but the question which forces itself upon thoughtful men in all lands is: Why should men leave great fortunes to their children? If this is done from affection, is it not misguided affection? Observation teaches that, generally speaking, it is not well for the children that they should be so burdened. Neither is it well for the State. Beyond providing for the wife and daughters moderate sources of income, and very moderate allowances indeed, if any, for the sons, men may well hesitate, for it is no longer questionable that great sums bequeathed oftener work more for the injury than for the good of the recipients. Wise men will soon conclude that, for the best interests of the members of their families and of the State, such bequests are an improper use of their means.

It is not suggested that men who have failed to educate their sons to earn a livelihood cast them adrift in poverty. If any man has seen fit to rear his sons with a view to their living idle lives, or, what is highly commendable, has instilled in them the sentiment that they are in a position to labor for public ends without reference to pecuniary considerations, then, of course, the duty of the parent is to see that such are provided for *in moderation.* There are instances of millionaires' sons unspoiled by wealth, who, being rich, still perform great services in the community. Such are the very salt of the earth, as valuable as, unfortunately, they are rare; still it is not the exception, but the rule, that men must regard, and, looking at the usual result of enormous sums conferred upon legatees, the thoughtful man must shortly say, "I would as soon leave to my son a curse as the almighty dollar," and admit to himself that it is not the welfare of the children, but family pride, which inspires these enormous legacies.

As to the second mode, that of leaving wealth at death for public uses, it may be said that this is only a means for the disposal of wealth, provided a man is content to wait until he is dead before he becomes of much good in the world. Knowledge of the results of legacies bequeathed is not calculated to inspire the brightest hopes of much posthumous good being accomplished. The cases are not few in which the real object sought by the testator is not attained, nor are they few in which his real wishes are thwarted. In many cases the bequests are so used as to become only monuments of his folly. It is well to remember that it requires the exercise of no less ability than that which acquired the wealth to use it so as to be really beneficial to the community. Besides this, it may fairly be said that no man is to be extolled for doing what he cannot help doing, nor is he to be thanked by the community to which he only leaves wealth at death. Men who leave vast sums in this way may fairly be thought men who would not have left it at all, had they been able to take it with them. The memories of such cannot be held in grateful remembrance, for there is no grace in their gifts. It is not to be wondered at that such bequests seem so generally to lack the blessing.

The growing disposition to tax more and more heavily large estates left at death is a cheering indication of the growth of a salutary change in public opinion. The State of Pennsylvania now takes—subject to some exceptions—one-tenth of the property left by its citizens. . . . Of all forms of taxation, this seems the wisest. Men who continue hoarding great sums all their lives, the proper use of which for public ends would work good to the community, should be made to feel that the community, in the form of the State, cannot thus be deprived of its proper share. By taxing estates heavily at death the State marks its condemnation of the selfish millionaire's unworthy life.

It is desirable that nations should go much further in this direction. Indeed, it is difficult to set bounds to the share of a rich man's estate which should go at his death to the public through the agency of the State, and by all means such taxes should be graduated, beginning at nothing upon moderate sums to dependents, and increasing rapidly as the amounts swell, until of the millionaire's hoard, as of Shylock's, at least

The other half
Comes to the privy coffer of the state.

This policy would work powerfully to induce the rich man to attend to the administration of wealth during his life, which is the end that society should always have in view, as being that by far the most fruitful for the people. Nor need it be feared that this policy would sap the root of enterprise and render men less anxious to accumulate, for to the class whose ambition it is to leave great fortunes and be talked about after their death, it will attract even more attention, and, indeed, be a somewhat nobler ambition to have enormous sums paid over to the state from their fortunes.

There remains, then, only one mode of using great fortunes; but in this we have the true antidote for the temporary unequal distribution of wealth, the reconciliation of the rich and the poor—a reign of harmony—another ideal, differing, indeed, from that of the Communist in requiring only the further evolution of existing conditions, not the total overthrow of our civilization. It is founded upon the present most intense individualism, and the race is prepared to put it in practice by degrees whenever it pleases. . . .

This, then, is held to be the duty of the man of Wealth: First, to set an example of modest, unostentatious living, shunning display or extravagance; to provide moderately for the legitimate wants of those dependent upon him; and after doing so to consider all surplus revenues which come to him simply as trust funds, which he is called upon to administer, and strictly bound as a matter of duty to

administer in the manner which, in his judgment, is best calculated
to produce the most beneficial results for the community—the man
of wealth thus becoming the mere agent and trustee for his poorer
brethen, bringing to their service his superior wisdom, experience,
and ability to administer, doing for them better than they would or
could do for themselves.

. . . It were better for mankind that the millions of the rich were
thrown into the sea than so spent as to encourage the slothful, the
drunken, the unworthy. Of every thousand dollars spent in so called
charity to-day, it is probable that $950 is unwisely spent, so spent,
indeed, as to produce the very evils which it proposes to mitigate
or cure. A well-known writer of philosophic books admitted the
other day that he had given a quarter of a dollar to a man who
approached him as he was coming to visit the house of his friend.
He knew nothing of the habits of this beggar, knew not the use that
would be made of this money, although he had every reason to
suspect that it would be spent improperly. This man professed to be
a disciple of Herbert Spencer; yet the quarter-dollar given that
night will probably work more injury than all the money which its
thoughtless donor will ever be able to give in true charity will do
good. He only gratified his own feelings, saved himself from annoy-
ance—and this was probably one of the most selfish and very worst
actions of his life, for in all respects he is most worthy.
    In bestowing charity, the main consideration should be to help
those who will help themselves; to provide part of the means by
which those who desire to improve may do so; to give those who
desire to rise the aids by which they may rise; to assist, but rarely
or never to do all. Neither the individual nor the race is improved
by alms-giving. Those worthy of assistance, except in rare cases,
seldom require assistance. The really valuable men of the race
never do, except in cases of accident or sudden change. Every one
has, of course, cases of individuals brought to his own knowledge
where temporary assistance can do genuine good, and these he will
not overlook. But the amount which can be wisely given by the
individual for individuals is necessarily limited by his lack of knowledge of the circumstances connected with each. He is the only true
reformer who is as careful and as anxious not to aid the unworthy
as he is to aid the worthy, and, perhaps, even more so, for in alms-
giving more injury is probably done by rewarding vice than by
relieving virtue.
    [Andrew Carnegie, "Wealth," *North American Review* 148, no.
391 (June 1889): 657–663]

Document 2. Russell Conwell Encourages Christians to Obtain Wealth

In the sermon "Acres of Diamonds,"
which Russell Conwell delivered more than
6,000 times, he advised Christians to use
their talent and energy to obtain wealth.

. . . I say you ought to be rich; you have no right to be poor.
. . . You ought to be rich. But persons with certain religious prejudice will ask, "How can you spend your time advising the rising

generation to give their time to getting money—dollars and cents—the commercial spirit?"

Yet I must say that you ought to spend time getting rich. You and I know there are some things more valuable than money; of course, we do. Ah, yes! By a heart made unspeakably sad by a grave on which the autumn leaves now fall, I know there are some things higher and grander and sublimer than money. Well does the man know, who has suffered, that there are some things sweeter and holier and more sacred than gold. Nevertheless, the man of common sense also knows that there is not one of those things that is not greatly enhanced by the use of money. Money is power. . . . Money is power; money has powers; and for a man to say, "I do not want money," is to say, "I do not wish to do any good to my fellowmen." It is absurd thus to talk. It is absurd to disconnect them. This is a wonderfully great life, and you ought to spend your time getting money, because of the power there is in money. And yet this religious prejudice is so great that some people think it is a great honor to be one of God's poor. . . . We ought to get rich if we can by honorable and Christian methods, and these are the only methods that sweep us quickly toward the goal of riches.

I remember, not many years ago a young theological student who came into my office and said to me that he thought it was his duty to come in and "labor with me." I asked what had happened, and he said: "I feel it is my duty to come in and speak to you, sir, and say that the Holy Scriptures declare that money is the root of all evil." I asked him where he found that saying, and he said he found it in the Bible. . . . So he took the Bible and read it: "The *love* of money is the root of all evil." . . . Oh, that is it. It is the worship of the means instead of the end, though you cannot reach the end without the means. When a man makes an idol of the money instead of the purposes for which it may be used, when he squeezes the dollar until the eagle squeals, then it is made the root of all evil. Think, if you only had the money, what you could do for your wife, your child, and for your home and your city.

[Agnes Rush Burr, *Russell H. Conwell, Founder of the Institutional Church in America: The Work and the Man* (Philadelphia: The John C. Winston Co., 1905), pp. 324–326]

Questions for Reflection

Has Carnegie listed all the methods for the disposal of fortunes? Would most wealthy people today agree with his notions of how to treat members of the family? How do you react to his notion of using the inheritance tax? Does it appear to you that most very wealthy people today follow his dictates for modest living? Is Carnegie right about the harm of almsgiving? What appear to be the sources for Carnegie's ideas? Are his concepts valid today or were they appropriate only for the nineteenth century, if that?

How does Russell Conwell's sermon reflect attitudes similar to Carnegie's? Is Conwell providing an appropriate reflection of the ethic of modern Christianity? How would Conwell's ideas have been received by the wealthy people of his era? Why? Based on a reading of this portion of Conwell's sermon, how would you define the "Gospel of Wealth"?

ANSWERS TO MULTIPLE-CHOICE
AND TRUE-FALSE QUESTIONS

Multiple-Choice Questions

1-D, 2-D, 3-A, 4-C, 5-B, 6-C, 7-A, 8-D

True-False Questions

1-F, 2-T, 3-T, 4-F, 5-F, 6-F, 7-T, 8-F

20

THE EMERGENCE OF MODERN AMERICA

CHAPTER OBJECTIVES

After you complete the reading and study of this chapter you should be able to

1. Discuss the important intellectual trends in the period 1877–1890.
2. Describe city growth in the late nineteenth century.
3. Account for the new immigration and the reaction that it engendered.
4. Trace major developments in higher education after the Civil War.
5. Explain the concepts of Social Darwinism and Reform Darwinism.
6. Describe the local color, realist, and naturalist movements in literature.
7. Explain the social gospel and describe its manifestations.

CHAPTER OUTLINE

I. Urbanization
   A. Urbanization reflected in westward migration
   B. Factors important to urban prowess
   C. Characteristics of the new urban scene
   D. Vertical and horizontal growth of cities
      1. Development of elevators
      2. Introduction of cast-iron and steel-frame construction
      3. Development of electric streetcars
   E. City problems
      1. Tenements
      2. Health
      3. City services
   F. Role of city boss
   G. Lure of the city
II. The new immigration
   A. Reasons for emigration to America
   B. Nature of the new immigrants
   C. Ellis Island
      1. scale of operation
      2. reception of immigrants
   D. The immigrants' experiences
   E. The nativist response
      1. Reasons for objection to new immigrants
      2. Rise of American Protective Association
   F. Efforts at immigration restriction
      1. Legislation
      2. Treatment of Chinese on West Coast
III. Growth of education
   A. Indication of the spread of schooling
   B. Developments in higher education
      1. Growth of colleges
      2. Growth of the elective system

3. Expansion of opportunities for women
4. Development of graduate schools
C. The rise of professionalism
1. Nature of the movement
2. Fields developed

IV. Theories of social change
A. Darwinism
1. Darwin's ideas and their implications
2. Social Darwinism
a. Herbert Spencer's contributions
b. William Graham Sumner's contributions
3. Lester Frank Ward and Reform Darwinism
B. Developments in other fields of learning
1. Developments in history
2. Pragmatism
a. Ideas of William James
b. John Dewey and instrumentalism

V. Realism in American literature
A. The local colorists
1. Sarah Orne Jewett
2. George Washington Cable
3. Joel Chandler Harris
B. Mark Twain
C. William Dean Howells
D. Henry James

E. Literary naturalism
1. Frank Norris
2. Stephen Crane
3. Jack London
4. Theodore Dreiser

VI. Social critics
A. Henry George and the single tax
B. Henry Demarest Lloyd and cooperation
C. Thorstein Veblen and conspicuous consumption

VII. The religious response: social gospel
A. Abandonment of inner-city churches
B. Development of the institutional church
1. YMCA and the Salvation Army
2. Other facilities
C. Washington Gladden
D. Catholic responses to modernity

VIII. Early efforts at urban reform
A. The settlement house movement
B. Women's rights
1. Growth of the female labor force
2. Women's suffrage
a. Conflicts in the movement
b. Gains in the states
3. Other women's efforts
C. The status of laissez-faire government at the end of the century

KEY ITEMS OF CHRONOLOGY

Founding of the Johns Hopkins University	1876
Henry George's *Progress and Poverty*	1879
Publication of *Dynamic Sociology*	1883
Publication of *Huckleberry Finn*	1883
First electric elevator	1889
Electric streetcar systems in cities	1890s
Publication of *Maggie: A Girl of the Streets*	1893
Veblen's *The Theory of the Leisure Class*	1899

TERMS TO MASTER

Listed below are some important terms or people with which you should be familiar after you complete the study of this chapter. Explain the significance of each name or term.

1. Frederick Law Olmstead
2. "streetcar suburbs"
3. the "new" immigration
4. American Protective Association
5. The Johns Hopkins University
6. professionalism
7. Social Darwinism
8. William Graham Sumner
9. Lester Frank Ward
10. "scientific" history
11. pragmatism
12. John Dewey
13. local color movement
14. Henry James
15. naturalism
16. Henry George
17. social gospel
18. settlement houses
19. Susan B. Anthony

VOCABULARY BUILDING

Listed below are some words used in this chapter. Look up each in your dictionary.

1. tenement
2. sinister
3. beguile
4. nativism
5. accreditation
6. inviolable
7. ameliorate
8. milieu
9. folkways
10. pecuniary

EXERCISES FOR UNDERSTANDING

When you have completed the reading of the chapter, answer each of the following questions. If you have difficulty, go back and reread the section of the chapter related to the question.

Multiple-Choice Questions

Select the letter of the response that best completes the statement.

1. The most urbanized population in the United States by 1900 was
   A. along the East Coast.
   B. on the Pacific Coast.
   C. in the South.
   D. in the Midwest.

2. Urban political machines did *not*
   A. help immigrants cope with city life.
   B. operate honestly.
   C. provide needed city services.
   D. aid the poor and needy.

3. Most immigrants probably came to the United States because of
   A. famine and poverty in Europe.
   B. religious and ethnic persecution in their home countries.
   C. wars in Europe.
   D. the chance for jobs and land in America.

4. An important new trend in higher education after the Civil War was
   A. coeducation.
   B. the development of a varied curriculum.
   C. the rise of graduate schools.
   D. the creation of land-grant colleges.

5. Lester Frank Ward stressed
   A. the power of folkways in determining social conditions.
   B. the potential of human intelligence in planning change.
   C. the importance of heredity in human progress.
   D. the similarity of social evolution and biological evolution.

6. Henry George believed that all social ills could be solved by
   A. an income tax.
   B. socialization of all private property.
   C. a tax on unearned wealth coming from land ownership.
   D. a tax on the number of windows in a house.

7. The social gospel of Washington Gladden encouraged
   A. assistance to middle-class Christians.
   B. a focus on personal sins and saving souls.
   C. community services and helping the poor.
   D. the laissez-faire business philosophy.

8. A leader in the settlement house movement was
   A. Thorstein Veblen.
   B. William Dean Howells.
   C. Jane Addams.
   D. Susan B. Anthony.

True-False Questions

Indicate whether each statement is true or false.

1. After the Civil War, more people moved to the frontier than to cities.
2. Between 1892 and 1954, twelve million immigrants entered the United States at Ellis Island.

3. From 1870 to 1890, the American college student population tripled.
4. Social Darwinism supported government regulation of business.
5. *The Theory of the Leisure Class* was written by Henry Demarest Lloyd.
6. Women's suffrage was achieved first in the urban states of the Northwest.
7. Railroads in the late-nineteenth century were effectively regulated by state laws strongly enforced by judges.

Essay Questions

1. What factors fueled the growth of cities in the late 1800s?
2. How did native-born Americans respond to the influx of the "new" immigrants?
3. Compare and contrast the policies of social Darwinism and reform Darwinism regarding such public issues as public education and regulation of business.
4. Describe the Social Gospel movement and assess its impact.
5. What characterized the local color, realist, and naturalist schools of literature in America?

DOCUMENT

Circumstances of Typical Illinois Working Families

In 1884 the Illinois Bureau of Labor Statistics conducted a survey of typical laboring families. The survey included over 2,000 families, of whom 167 were selected for detailed accounts. Excerpted here are the accounts of eight families diverse in occupation, income, and circumstances.

> In order to present a closer view of the manner of living, the surroundings, habits, tastes and daily diet of the Illinois workingman of to-day, under various circumstances and conditions, and to afford a more definite impression as to the details of his environment than can be obtained from the mere contemplation of columns of figures, we transcribe, for a limited number of representative families, their entire record, as procured by our agents, together with the notes of observation, made at the time of the visit. . . .
>
> This minute catalogue of the details governing the life of each family portrays more vividly than any mere array of figures can the common current of daily life among the people. The extremes of condition and the average types are alike presented, and it may be seen, not only what manner of life ordinarily prevails with a given income, but also how some families, by thrift, temperance and pru-

dence, save money and increase their store, upon earnings which other families find insufficient for their support. . . .

No. 1   Baker   Scandinavian

Earnings—Of father $375
        Of daughter, aged eighteen   150
        Of son, aged fifteen   48
        Total $573

Condition—Family numbers 7—father, mother and five children, three girls and two boys. The girls aged eight, eleven and eighteen; boys, six and fifteen. The children attend school regularly. The house they occupy contains four rooms, and they pay $9 per month rent. The house is in an unhealthy and dirty locality, furnished very poorly, and kept in poor condition. The children, when out of school, pick fuel from the railroad tracks and accompanying lumber yards. The family are very ignorant, and live as the generality of the Swede race. Life insurance and trades unions are ignored.

Food—Breakfast—Coffee, bread, syrup.
      Dinner—Lunches, always.
      Supper—Meat, soup and bread.

Cost of Living—
    Rent $108
    Fuel   12
    Meat and groceries   200
    Clothing, boots and shoes, and dry goods   150
    Books, papers, etc.   3
    Sundries [miscellaneous items]   50
    Total $523

No. 23   Cigar Maker   French

Earnings—Of father $790

Condition—Family numbers 4—parents and two children, girl aged seven years and boy five. Live in house containing 6 rooms and pay for same rent at the rate of $10 per month. Both children attend school. Father carries some life insurance and belongs to trades union, and claims his wages this year are increased thereby about $200 over his wages of previous years, enabling them to live more comfortably, dress the children better, and eat more substantial and healthy food. Children healthy, bright and intelligent, and attend Sunday school. House is well furnished and has a small library. Live well and seem to be well satisfied, although their expenses equal their earnings.

Food—Breakfast—Coffee, bread, butter, milk, sugar and potatoes.
      Dinner—Tea, bread, butter, ham and eggs, poultry and dessert.
      Supper—Coffee, bread, butter, cheese, potatoes.

Cost of Living—
    Rent $120
    Fuel   35

Meat	100
Groceries	300
Clothing	75
Boots and shoes	15
Dry goods	20
Books, papers, etc.	8
Life insurance	17
Trades union	11
Sickness	80
Sundries	9
Total	$790

No. 65   Plumber   Scotch-American

Earnings—Of father $1,050

Condition—Family numbers 3—parents and one girl seven years old, who attends school. Occupy 3 rooms, for which they pay $13 per month rent; situation not very pleasant, but healthy; have had very little sickness. Rooms comfortably furnished. Family dress plainly, are below the average in intelligence, do not attend church or better class of public entertainments. The head of the family has employment fifty weeks during the year, and earns more than the average of wage-workers, which would indicate sobriety and industry, notwithstanding much of his leisure time is spent in beer-gardens and like places of amusement.

Food—Breakfast—Bread, butter, meat, potatoes, eggs, fruit.
         Dinner—Lunch.
         Supper—About the same as breakfast.

Cost of Living—

Rent	$156
Fuel	36
Meat	100
Groceries	200
Clothing	60
Boots and shoes	27
Dry goods	15
Books, papers, etc.	7
Sickness	10
Sundries	150
Total	$761

No. 77   Street-Car Conductor   American

Earnings—Of father $691

Condition—Family numbers 4—parents and two boys, aged two and four years. Father works 38 weeks in the year and 12 hours per day, and receives for his services an average of $2.60 per day. Occupies house containing 4 comfortable rooms. Husband belongs to trades union, but does not carry any life insurance. Father does not have steady employment the entire year, and has very unpleasant hours to work. Goes to work at 5 o'clock A.M., works about six hours, then lays off until 4 P.M., from which time he works until 11 P.M.

Food—Breakfast—Bread, steak, and coffee.
        Dinner—Bread, vegetables, meat and fish.
        Supper—Same as breakfast.

Cost of Living—

Rent	$120
Fuel	60
Meat and groceries	280
Clothing, boots and shoes and dry goods	150
Books, papers, etc.	15
Trades union	5
Sickness	20
Sundries	40
Total	$690

No. 100   Upholsterer   Bohemian

Earnings—Of father $420

Condition—Family numbers 8—husband, wife and six children, four girls and two boys, the former aged, respectively, one month, one and a half, three and nine years, the latter five and seven. One of the children attends school; the rest of them, that are old enough, pick up coal, and go to the fruit warehouses and collect decayed fruit and other spoiled food. The family eat poor and spoiled meats, and live miserably, but seem to grow fat on it, and have but very little sickness. House contains three rooms, into which the eight persons are huddled. They pay $6 per month for the house. Family is dirty and ignorant in the extreme. The stench from the rooms is as bad as that from the stock yards.

Food—Breakfast—Coffee and bread.
        Dinner—Soup and potatoes.
        Supper—Coffee and bread.

Cost of Living—

Rent	$72
Fuel	8
Meat and groceries	240
Clothing, boots and shoes	80
Dry goods	10
Sickness	10
Total	$420

No. 129   Coal Miner   Irish

Earnings—Of father $368
           Of son, 17 years of age   368
           Of son, 14 years of age   172
           Total $908

Condition—Family numbers 9—parents and seven children, five
boys and two girls, their ages ranging from two to seventeen years.
Three of these attend school, and the two oldest boys work in the
mines. Family occupy a house containing 3 rooms, with an addition
of a shanty, for which they pay $5 per month rent. Father is an
industrious and hard-working man, but only had thirty weeks work
during the year. He is a leader among his class, is a great reader,
belongs to temperance society, life insurance society, and trades
union. Family healthy, and members of a church. They work half
an acre of land, and raise vegetables enough for family use. They
are making payments on a lot, sewing machine and back debts.

Food—Breakfast—Bread, butter, meat and coffee.
          Dinner—Bread, butter, cheese or meat and tea.
          Supper—Meat, potatoes, vegetables, bread, butter, pie and
               tea.

Cost of Living—
          Rent $60
          Fuel   15
          Meat   120
          Groceries   360
          Clothing   170
          Boots, shoes and dry goods   63
          Books, papers, etc.   8
          Life insurance   30
          Trades union   5
          Sickness   4
          Sundries   63
               Total $898

No. 142   Laborer   American

Earnings—Of father $324

Condition—Family numbers 5—parents and three children, all
boys, aged two, five and nine years respectively. Family occupy a
house containing 3 rooms, situated in a very unhealthy locality,
miserable surroundings, in the vicinity of a slough. Have a few
chairs, bedstead, two poor stoves, but no carpets. Family·poorly
dressed; father works in saw mill; one cent per hour is retained by
his employers on condition that he loses it if he leaves their service
before the season closes. Father claims to have lost this 11 cts per
day for the year 1881, as he had three of his fingers cut off, and could
not work the season out.

Food—Breakfast—Bread, butter and coffee.
  Dinner—Bread, meat and coffee.
  Supper—Bread, butter, coffee and potatoes.

Cost of Living—
Rent	$48
Fuel	22
Meat and groceries	220
Clothing, boots, shoes and dry goods	30
Sickness	35
Total	$355

No. 165   Superintendent, Glass Works   American

Earnings—Of father $1,010
  Of son, 17 years old   612
  Of son, 15 years old   180
  Total $1,802

Condition—Family numbers 8—parents and six children, three boys, aged eight, sixteen and eighteen years, and three girls, aged one, five and eleven years. Two of the children attend school. Family occupy a comfortable house, containing 7 rooms, for which they pay a rental of $25 per month. Floors are all carpeted. Have piano and sewing machine. Family intelligent, and attend church regularly. They manage to save but little of their earnings. Father receives $125 per month, but only worked thirty-six weeks of the past year. He carries no life insurance.

Food—Breakfast—Bread, meat, coffee, and potatoes.
  Dinner—Meats, vegetables, coffee and fruits.
  Supper—Meat, potatoes, tea and fruits.

Cost of Living—
Rent	$300
Fuel	40
Meat	200
Groceries	300
Clothing	125
Boots and shoes	75
Dry goods	100
Books, papers, etc.	20
Sickness	100
Sundries	150
Total	$1,410

[From *Third Biennial Report of the Bureau of Labor Statistics of Illinois* (Springfield, Ill.: State Printer and Binder, 1884), pp. 357–358, 361, 365, 379, 383, 391, 401, 405, 413]

Questions for Reflection

Analyze carefully the different amounts spent by each family on the major catagories. What factors seem to affect family income? Which categories seem to increase most as families become more affluent? After examining this information, how much would you estimate to be the minimum amount required for a family to live comfortably?

The comments about family lifestyles were made by investigators who visited the families. What evidence can you cite to show the basic assumptions or attitudes about family life which were likely held by these investigators?

From all this information, what conclusions can you draw about family life among the working class in Illinois in the 1880s?

ANSWERS TO MULTIPLE-CHOICE AND TRUE-FALSE QUESTIONS

Multiple-Choice Questions

1-B, 2-B, 3-D, 4-C, 5-B, 6-C, 7-C, 8-C

True-False Questions

1-F, 2-T, 3-T, 4-F, 5-F, 6-F, 7-F

21

GILDED AGE POLITICS
AND AGRARIAN REVOLT

CHAPTER OBJECTIVES

After you complete the reading and study of this chapter you should be able to

1. Describe the major features of politics in the late-nineteenth century.
2. Describe the political alignments and issues in the "third political system."
3. Explain the major issues in the presidential elections of 1888, 1892, and 1896.
4. Account for the rise of the farmers' protest movement of the 1890s.
5. Explain the impact of populism on the American scene.

CHAPTER OUTLINE

I. Nature of Gilded Age politics
  A. National political parties
    1. Evasion of issues
    2. Some disagreement on tariff
    3. Even division between parties in popular vote (1868–1912)
    4. No strong president
    5. Importance of patronage
  B. The voters
    1. High voter participation
    2. Belief in reality of issues
    3. Intense cultural conflicts
  C. Ethnic and religious divisions
    1. Republicans
    2. Democrats
    3. Issues
      a. Nativism
      b. Prohibition
II. The Hayes administration
  A. Hayes's background
  B. Divided Republicans
    1. Stalwarts and Conkling
    2. Half-Breeds and Blaine
  C. Support for civil service reform
  D. Hayes's limited version of government
III. The election of 1880
  A. Republican nomination
    1. The Grant candidacy
    2. Garfield's nomination as a dark horse
  B. Democratic nomination of Winfield Scott Hancock
  C. Closest election results of the century
IV. The Garfield-Arthur administration
  A. Garfield's background and his assassination
  B. Arthur's background
  C. His strong actions as president
    1. Support of Pendleton Civil Service Act, 1883

2. Support for tariff reduction
  a. Effects of treasury surplus
  b. Nature of the Mongrel Tariff of 1883
D. Scurrilous campaign of 1884
  1. Reasons Arthur was not a candidate
  2. Republican nomination of Blaine and Logan
    a. Blaine's background
    b. Effect of Mulligan letters
    c. Emergence of "Mugwumps"
  3. Democratic nomination of Cleveland
    a. Cleveland's political background
    b. His illegitimate child
    c. Concept of "Rum, Romanism, and Rebellion"
  4. Election results

V. Cleveland's presidency
  A. Cleveland's view of the role of government
  B. His actions on civil service
  C. His stand against veterans' pensions
  D. The Interstate Commerce Act
  E. His stand for tariff reform
  F. Election of 1888
    1. Cleveland renominated
    2. Republican nomination of Benjamin Harrison
    3. Campaign focuses on the tariff
    4. Personal attacks
    5. Results

VI. Republican reform under Harrison
  A. Treatment of veterans
  B. Republican control of Congress, 1889–1891
    1. Passage of Sherman Antitrust Act, 1890
    2. Sherman Silver Purchase Act, 1890
    3. Effect of McKinley Tariff, 1890
  C. Democratic congressional victories of 1890
    1. Ostensible reaction to heavy spending of Republicans
    2. Impact on the election of prohibition and social issues

VII. Problems of farmers
  A. Worsening economic and social conditions
    1. Causes for declining agricultural prices
      a. Overproduction
      b. Worldwide competition
    2. The railroads as villains
    3. Effects of the tariff on farmers
    4. Problems of currency deflation
    5. Problems of geography and climate
    6. Isolation of farmers
  B. Development of Patrons of Husbandry
    1. Development of the Grange
    2. Effects of Granger political activity
  C. Rise of the Greenback Party
  D. Emergence of Farmers' Alliances
    1. Cooperative ideal
    2. Economic program
    3. Entry into politics
    4. Mary Elizabeth Lease and Jerry Simpson
  E. The Populist Party
    1. Development of the party
    2. Platform stands
    3. Presidential nominees
    4. Victory of Cleveland in 1892

VIII. Depression of 1893
  A. Nature of the depression
  B. Reactions to the depression
  C. Results of the 1894 elections

IX. Focus on silver
  A. The gold drain
  B. Agitation for free silver
  C. Effect on nominations of 1896
    1. Republican actions
    2. Democratic candidate
    3. Populist position
  D. Campaign of 1896 and its results
  E. The postelection shift to gold

KEY ITEMS OF CHRONOLOGY

Patrons of Husbandry founded	1867
Hayes administration	1877–1881
Munn v. Illinois	1877
Garfield administration	March–September 1881
Arthur administration	September 1881–1885
Pendleton Civil Service Act	1883
Mongrel Tariff Act	1883
Cleveland administrations 1893–1897	1885–1889;
Interstate Commerce Act	1887
Benjamin Harrison administration	1889–1893
Sherman Anti-Trust Act	1890
Sherman Silver Purchase Act	1890
McKinley Tariff Act	1890
Populist Party founded	1892
Economic depression	1893
McKinley administrations	1897–1901

TERMS TO MASTER

Listed below are some important terms or people with which you should be familiar after you complete the study of this chapter. Explain the significance of each name or term.

1. Stalwarts and Half-Breeds
2. Bland-Allison Act
3. Pendleton Civil Service Act (1883)
4. "Mongrel Tariff" of 1883
5. James G. Blaine
6. Mugwumps
7. *Wabash Railroad v. Illinois*
8. Sherman Anti-Trust Act
9. Sherman Silver Purchase Act
10. McKinley Tariff
11. "free and unlimited coinage of silver"
12. Patrons of Husbandry
13. Farmers' Alliances
14. Populist party
15. Jacob S. Coxey
16. William Jennings Bryan

VOCABULARY BUILDING

Listed below are some words used in this chapter. Look up each word in your dictionary.

1. jaundiced
2. bipartisan
3. static
4. disfranchisement
5. electorate
6. besmirched
7. sartorial
8. sop
9. scurrilous
10. consummate
11. commodity
12. fester

EXERCISES FOR UNDERSTANDING

When you have completed reading the chapter, answer each of the following questions. If you have difficulty, go back and reread the section of the chapter related to the question.

Multiple-Choice Questions

Select the letter of the response that best completes the statement.

1. The political parties from 1870 to 1896 generally
   A. disagreed about the issue of civil service reform.
   B. pursued a policy of evasion on all issues.
   C. most closely agreed with each other on the issue of the tariff.
   D. disagreed most strongly over the regulation of business.

2. The Republican party generally consisted of
   A. southern whites, political insiders, and immigrants.
   B. Catholics, reformers, and prohibitionists.
   C. nativists, Catholics, and blacks.
   D. moral reformers, Protestants, and political insiders.

3. The Pendleton Civil Service Act provided that
   A. most government jobs would be filled on merit.
   B. presidents could increase the jobs covered by civil service.
   C. Congress had to approve all civil service appointees.
   D. presidents could not appoint any political friends to office.

4. As president, Cleveland did *not*
   A. try to add pensions for Confederate veterans.
   B. restore to the public domain exploited public lands in the West.
   C. work to reduce the tariff.
   D. create an agency to regulate railroads and other interstate commerce.

5. The Sherman Silver Purchase Act of 1890
   A. reduced the government's purchases of silver.
   B. led to the inflation desired by farmers.
   C. worried eastern business and financial groups.
   D. did all of the above

6. The basic problem of farmers in the late-nineteenth century was

   A. high rates charged by railroads.
   B. overproduction of agricultural products.
   C. inflation.
   D. high prices for manufactured goods caused by high tariffs.

7. The Populist party demanded
   A. government ownership of railroads.
   B. coinage of silver.
   C. an income tax.
   D. all of the above

8. The Democratic candidate for president in 1896 was
   A. William Jennings Bryan.
   B. James G. Blaine.
   C. Grover Cleveland.
   D. William McKinley.

True-False Questions

Indicate whether each statement is true or false.

1. The Republican party clearly dominated American politics in the Gilded Age.
2. Party loyalty and voter turnout in the Gilded Age were primarily motivated by intense cultural conflicts among ethnic groups.
3. President Arthur supported *both* civil service reform and tariff reform.
4. "Rum, Romanism, and Rebellion" referred to the Republican party in the 1888 election.
5. The key issue in the 1888 election was the tariff.
6. Republicans suffered severe losses in the 1890 elections.
7. In the 1870s the Grangers primarily sought inflation of the currency.
8. "You shall not crucify mankind upon a cross of gold," said Grover Cleveland.

Essay Questions

1. Describe the difference between the Democratic party and the Republican party in the late-nineteenth century. Pay special attention to their stands on the issues and the nature of their supporters.
2. Of the presidents between 1876 and 1896, which would you say was the most successful? Explain your response.

3. Explain why the coinage of silver was an important issue in the late-nineteenth century.
4. What issues divided the Republicans in the 1870s and 1880s?

5. What caused the farmers' problems in the Gilded Age? Explain.
6. Describe the programs advocated by the Populist party in the 1890s. How would you judge their success?

DOCUMENT

The Omaha Platform of the Populist Party

The platform adopted by the Populist party in 1892 shows what the Populists thought was wrong with America and how they proposed to remedy these ills.

National People's Party Platform

Assembled upon the 116th anniversary of the Declaration of Independence, the People's Party of America, in their first national convention, invoking upon their action the blessing of Almighty God, put forth in the name and on behalf of the people of this country, the following preamble and declaration of principles:

Preamble

The conditions which surround us best justify our co-operation; we meet in the midst of a nation brought to the verge of moral, political, and material ruin. Corruption dominates the ballot-box, the Legislatures, the Congress, and touches even the ermine of the bench. The people are demoralized; most of the States have been compelled to isolate the voters at the polling places to prevent universal intimidation and bribery. The newspapers are largely subsidized or muzzled, public opinion silenced, business prostrated, homes covered with mortgages, labor impoverished, and the land concentrating in the hands of capitalists. The urban workmen are denied the right to organize for self-protection, imported pauperized labor beats down their wages, a hireling standing army, unrecognized by our laws, is established to shoot them down, and they are rapidly degenerating into European conditions. The fruits of the toil of millions are boldly stolen to build up colossal fortunes for a few, unprecedented in the history of mankind; and the possessors of those, in turn, despise the Republic and endanger liberty. From the same prolific womb of governmental injustice we breed the two great classes—tramps and millionaires.

The national power to create money is appropriated to enrich bondholders; a vast public debt payable in legal tender currency has been funded into gold-bearing bonds, thereby adding millions to the burdens of the people.

Silver, which has been accepted as coin since the dawn of history, has been demonetized to add to the purchasing power of gold by decreasing the value of all forms of property as well as human labor, and the supply of currency is purposely abridged to fatten usurers, bankrupt enterprise, and enslave industry. A vast conspiracy against mankind has been organized on two continents, and it is rapidly taking possession of the world. If not met and overthrown at once it forebodes terrible social convulsions, the destruction of civilization, or the establishment of an absolute despotism.

We have witnessed for more than a quarter of a century the struggles of the two great political parties for power and plunder, while grievous wrongs have been inflicted upon the suffering people. We charge that the controlling influences dominating both these parties have permitted the existing dreadful conditions to develop without serious effort to prevent or restrain them. Neither do they now promise us any substantial reform. They have agreed together to ignore, in the coming campaign, every issue but one. They propose to drown the outcries of a plundered people with the uproar of a sham battle over the tariff, so that capitalists, corporations, national banks, rings, trusts, watered stock, the demonetization of silver and the oppressions of the usurers may all be lost sight of. They propose to sacrifice our homes, lives, and children on the altar of mammon; to destroy the multitude in order to secure corruption funds from the millionaires.

Assembled on the anniversary of the birthday of the nation, and filled with the spirit of the grand general and chief who established our independence, we seek to restore the government of the Republic to the hands of "the plain people," with which class it originated. We assert our purposes to be identical with the purposes of the National Constitution; to form a more perfect union and establish justice, insure domestic tranquility, provide for the common defence, promote the general welfare, and secure the blessings of liberty for ourselves and our posterity.

We declare that this Republic can only endure as a free government while built upon the love of the whole people for each other and for the nation; that it cannot be pinned together by bayonets; that the civil war is over, and that every passion and resentment which grew out of it must die with it, and that we must be in fact, as we are in name, one united brotherhood of free men.

Our country finds itself confronted by conditions for which there is no precedent in the history of the world; our annual agricultural productions amount to billions of dollars in value, which must, within a few weeks or months, be exchanged for billions of dollars' worth of commodities consumed in their production; the existing currency supply is wholly inadequate to make this exchange; the results are falling prices, the formation of combines and rings, the impoverishment of the producing class. We pledge ourselves that if given power we will labor to correct these evils by wise and reasonable legislation, in accordance with the terms of our platform.

We believe that the power of government—in other words, of the people—should be expanded (as in the case of the postal service) as rapidly and as far as the good sense of an intelligent people and the teachings of experience shall justify, to the end that oppression, injustice, and poverty shall eventually cease in the land.

While our sympathies as a party of reform are naturally upon the side of every proposition which will tend to make men intelligent, virtuous, and temperate, we nevertheless regard these questions, important as they are, as secondary to the great issues now pressing for solution, and upon which not only our individual prosperity but the very existence of free institutions depend; and we ask all men to first help us to determine whether we are to have a republic to administer before we differ as to the conditions upon which it is to be administered, believing that the forces of reform this day organized will never cease to move forward until every wrong is remedied and equal rights and equal privileges securely established for all the men and women of this country.

Platform

We declare, therefore—

First.—That the union of the labor forces of the United States this day consummated shall be permanent and perpetual; may its spirit enter into all hearts for the salvation of the Republic and the uplifting of mankind.

Second.—Wealth belongs to him who creates it, and every dollar taken from industry without an equivalent is robbery. "If any will not work, neither shall he eat." The interests of rural and civic labor are the same; their enemies are identical.

Third.—We believe that the time has come when the railroad corporations will either own the people or the people must own the railroads, and should the government enter upon the work of owning and managing all railroads, we should favor an amendment to the Constitution by which all persons engaged in the government service shall be placed under a civil-service regulation of the most rigid character, so as to prevent the increase of the power of the national administration by the use of such additional government employes.

Finance.—We demand a national currency safe, sound, and flexible, issued by the general government only, a full legal tender for all debts, public and private, and that without the use of banking corporations, a just, equitable, and efficient means of distribution direct to the people, at a tax not to exceed 2 per cent per annum, to be provided as set forth in the sub-treasury plan of the Farmers' Alliance, or a better system; also by payments in discharge of its obligations for public improvements.

1. We demand free and unlimited coinage of silver and gold at the present legal ratio of 16 to 1.

2. We demand that the amount of circulating medium be speedily increased to not less than $50 per capita.

3. We demand a graduated income tax.

4. We believe that the money of the country should be kept as much as possible in the hands of the people, and hence we demand that all State and national revenues shall be limited to the necessary expenses of the government, economically and honestly administered.

5. We demand that postal savings banks be established by the government for the safe deposit of the earnings of the people and to facilitate exchange.

Transportation.—Transportation being a means of exchange and a public necessity, the government should own and operate the railroads in the interest of the people. The telegraph, telephone, like the post-office system, being a necessity for the transmission of news, should be owned and operated by the government in the interest of the people.

Land.—The land, including all the natural sources of wealth, is the heritage of the people, and should not be monopolized for speculative purposes, and alien ownership of land should be prohibited. All land now held by railroads and other corporations in excess of their actual needs, and all lands now owned by aliens should be reclaimed by the government and held for actual settlers only.

Expression of Sentiments

Your Committee on Platform and Resolutions beg leave unanimously to report the following:

Whereas, Other questions have been presented for our consideration, we hereby submit the following, not as a part of the Platform of the People's Party, but as resolutions expressive of the sentiment of the Convention.

1. *Resolved,* That we demand a free ballot and a fair count in all elections, and pledge ourselves to secure it to every legal voter without Federal intervention, through the adoption by the States of the unperverted Australian or secret ballot system.

2. *Resolved,* That the revenue derived from a graduated income tax should be applied to the reduction of the burden of taxation now levied upon the domestic industries of this country.

3. *Resolved,* That we pledge our support to fair and liberal pensions to ex-Union soldiers and sailors.

4. *Resolved,* That we condemn the fallacy of protecting American labor under the present system, which opens our ports to the pauper and criminal classes of the world and crowds out our wage-earners; and we denounce the present ineffective laws against contract labor, and demand the further restriction of undesirable emigration.

5. *Resolved,* That we cordially sympathize with the efforts of organized workingmen to shorten the hours of labor, and demand a rigid enforcement of the existing eight-hour law on Government work, and ask that a penalty clause be added to the said law.

6. *Resolved,* That we regard the maintenance of a large standing army of mercenaries, known as the Pinkerton system, as a menance to our liberties, and we demand its abolition; and we condemn the recent invasion of the Territory of Wyoming by the hired assassins of plutocracy, assisted by Federal officers.

7. *Resolved,* That we commend to the favorable consideration of the people and the reform press the legislative system known as the initiative and referendum.

8. *Resolved,* That we favor a constitutional provision limiting the office of President and Vice-President to one term, and providing for the election of Senators of the United States by a direct vote of the people.

9. *Resolved,* That we oppose any subsidy or national aid to any private corporation for any purpose.

10. *Resolved,* That this convention sympathizes with the Knights of Labor and their righteous contest with the tyrannical combine of

clothing manufacturers of Rochester, and declare it to be the duty of all who hate tyranny and oppression to refuse to purchase the goods made by the said manufacturers, or to patronize any merchants who sell such goods.

[*The World Almanac,* 1893 (New York: Publisher, 1893), pp. 83–85, reprinted in *A Populist Reader,* edited by George B. Tindall (New York: Harper and Row, 1966), pp. 90–96]

Questions for Reflection

What ideas expressed in the preamble do you recognize from your study of this period? (For example, the "hireling standing army" refers to the Pinkerton detectives often used in cases of industrial violence.)

Which planks of the platform and expressions of sentiments were later enacted in one form or another?

ANSWERS TO MULTIPLE-CHOICE AND TRUE-FALSE QUESTIONS

Multiple-Choice Questions

1-B, 2-D, 3-B, 4-A, 5-C, 6-B, 7-D, 8-A

True-False Questions

1-F, 2-T, 3-T, 4-F, 5-T, 6-T, 7-F, 8-F

22

THE COURSE OF EMPIRE

CHAPTER OBJECTIVES

After you complete the reading and study of this chapter you should be able to

1. Explain why the United States entered upon a policy of imperialism.
2. Account for the outbreak of the Spanish-American War.
3. Explain the course of United States relations with Latin America during the late-nineteenth century and its impact on later relations with Latin America.
4. Contrast the arguments in 1899 for and against imperialism.
5. Explain the development of America's policy for dealing with its imperial possessions.
6. Account for the acquisition of the Panama Canal.
7. Assess the foreign policies of Theodore Roosevelt and William Howard Taft.

CHAPTER OUTLINE

I. Stirrings of imperialism
   A. Isolationism prior to the Civil War
   B. Seward's diplomacy
      1. Purchase of Alaska (1867)
   C. Expansionist visions in the Pacific
      1. Early whaling and missionary interests
      2. Treaty with Samoa
      3. Relations with Hawaii
         a. Early American settlements
         b. Reciprocal trade agreement of 1875
         c. Constitutional government
         d. Desire for annexation (1893)
         e. Hawaii proclaimed a republic (1894)

II. Motivation for imperialism
   A. Economic motivations
   B. Mahan's concept of sea power
   C. Social Darwinian justifications
      1. Concept of Social Darwinism
      2. Racial corollaries
   D. Religious justification

III. Development of the Spanish-American War
   A. Effects of American investments and tariffs
   B. Guerrilla warfare by revolutionaries
   C. Weyler's detention policy
   D. Role of the press in the war
      1. Contest between Hearst's *Journal* and Pulitzer's *World*
      2. Examples of yellow journalism
   E. Cleveland's efforts for compromise
   F. Spanish response to McKinley's stance
   G. Arousal of public opinion
      1. de Lôme letter (February 9, 1898)
      2. Sinking of the *Maine* (February 15, 1898)

H. The final moves to war
I. Motives for war

IV. Fighting the "splendid little war"
   A. Naval victory at Manila Bay
   B. Cuban blockade
      1. Problems of the army
      2. The Rough Riders
      3. Siege of Santiago
   C. Puerto Rican campaign
   D. Terms of the armistice

V. Developing and debating imperialism
   A. Negotiations for the Treaty of Paris
      (December 10)
      1. Cuban debt question
      2. Annexation of the Philippines
   B. Motives for annexation
   C. Terms of the treaty
   D. Other territorial acquisitions
   E. Debate over the treaty
      1. Anti-imperialist arguments
      2. Bryan's support
      3. Ratification (February 1899)
   F. Filipino insurrection
   G. Emergence of the Anti-Imperialist
      League (October 1899)

VI. Organizing the new acquisitions
   A. The Philippines under Taft
   B. Civil government for Puerto Rico
   C. Problems in Cuba
   D. Imperial rivalries and the Open Door
      Policy in the Far East
      1. The scramble for spheres of
         influence in China
      2. The Open Door Policy
         a. British initiatives
         b. Unilateral action

c. Policies of the Open-Door Note
d. Reactions of other nations
      3. The Boxer Rebellion
      4. Success of Hay's policy

VII. Rise of Theodore Roosevelt
   A. Election of 1900
      1. Democrats and imperialism
      2. Republican nominees
      3. Outcome of election
   B. McKinley's assassination
   C. TR's background and character
      1. Strenuous life
      2. Life in the West
      3. New York politics

VIII. TR's foreign policies
   A. The Panama Canal
      1. Negotiations with British and
         French
      2. Difficulties with Colombia
      3. Revolution in Panama
      4. Treaty with Panama
      5. Opening of Canal
   B. The Roosevelt Corollary
      1. Problems of debt collection
      2. Principles in new policy
   C. TR's role in the Russo-Japanese War
   D. American relations with Japan
      1. Agreements on Korea, China,
         and Philippines
      2. Racism
      3. "Gentlemen's Agreement" of
         1907
   E. The United States and Europe
      1. Conference at Algeciras
      2. Tour of the "Great White Fleet"

KEY ITEMS OF CHRONOLOGY

Purchase of Alaska	1867
Mahan's *The Influence of Seapower upon History*	1890
de Lôme letter revealed	February 9, 1898
Maine sunk	February 15, 1898
War formally declared between Spain and the United States	April 1898
Hawaii annexed	July 1898
Armistice	August 1898
Treaty of Paris	December 1898
Anti-Imperialist League formed	1899

Open Door Note	1899
Assassination of McKinley	1901
Panama Canal acquired	1903
Roosevelt Corollary announced	1904
"Gentlemen's Agreement" with Japan	1907

TERMS TO MASTER

Listed below are some important terms or people with which you should be familiar after you complete the study of this chapter. Explain the significance of each name or term.

1. William H. Seward
2. Alfred Thayer Mahan
3. John Fiske
4. Josiah Strong
5. yellow journalism
6. de Lôme letter
7. Teller Amendment
8. Platt Amendment
9. Open Door Policy
10. Boxer Rebellion
11. Panama Canal
12. Roosevelt Corollary
13. Portsmouth conference
14. "Gentlemen's Agreement"
15. "Great White fleet"

VOCABULARY BUILDING

Listed below are some words used in this chapter. Look up each word in your dictionary.

1. annexation
2. isthmian
3. sanction
4. chagrin
5. unilateral
6. reminiscent
7. euphoria
8. anarchist
9. prodigious
10. pristine

EXERCISES FOR UNDERSTANDING

When you have completed reading the chapter, answer each of the following questions. If you have difficulty, go back and reread the section of the chapter related to the question.

Multiple-Choice Questions

Select the letter of the response that best completes the statement.

1. The "new imperialism" of the 1890s especially stressed
   A. access to new markets.
   B. converting heathens to Christianity.
   C. annexing territory to the United States.
   D. military conquests of other nations.

2. The ideas of Charles Darwin were used by some, including John Fiske, to
   A. justify imperialism by all nations.
   B. support Anglo-Saxon dominance.
   C. criticize colonialism.
   D. advocate revolution by oppressed peoples.

3. According to the text, a key factor propelling the United States into the Spanish-American War was
   A. the desire of businessmen to control trade and manufacturing in Cuba.
   B. the hope of missionaries to convert the Cuban people.
   C. McKinley's desire to gain political support from his acquisitions.
   D. the frenzy of public opinion for war.

4. The Teller Amendment called for
   A. war against Spain and the Philippines.
   B. annexation of Hawaii and Cuba.
   C. unlimited immigration to the United States.
   D. none of the above

5. Anti-imperialist arguments after the Spanish-American War included all of the following *except*
   A. the white man's burden.
   B. traditional American isolationism.
   C. the incompatibility of "bananas and self-government".
   D. the cost of defending the Philippines.

6. The Platt Amendment
   A. gave women the right to vote in national elections.
   B. annexed Puerto Rico.
   C. limited the independence of the new Cuban government.
   D. gave the president expanded power in foreign affairs.

7. The proposal that each nation should have equal access to trade with China was known as the
   A. "Gentlemen's Agreement."
   B. Open Door Policy.
   C. Teller Amendment.
   D. white man's burden.

8. The Roosevelt Corollary
   A. extended the Open Door Policy to Cuba.
   B. applied the Monroe Doctrine to Hawaii.
   C. repudiated the Teller and Platt Amendments.
   D. did none of the above

True-False Questions

Indicate whether each statement is true or false.

1. In the 1880s the major field of United States overseas activity was the Pacific Ocean.
2. Henry Cabot Lodge wrote *The Influence of Sea Power Upon History.*
3. The United States sided with the rebel Valeriano Weyler in the Cuban revolution.
4. The de Lôme letter explained why the *Maine* had been sunk.
5. The toughest question in American foreign policy in the 1890s involved the Philippines.
6. By 1920 both Puerto Rico and the Philippines had gained complete independence from the United States.
7. In the Russo-Japanese War the United States fought with the Japanese.
8. Theodore Roosevelt won a Nobel Prize for his work at the Portsmouth and Algeciras conferences.

Essay Questions

1. Describe three arguments Americans used to justify their imperialism in the late-nineteenth century.
2. What were the various factors that caused the Spanish-American War?
3. Discuss the arguments for and against acquisition of the Philippines.
4. Explain the Open-Door Policy and its effects.
5. How did United States policy in Latin America change between 1890 and 1912?
6. Trace developments leading to the acquisition of the Panama Canal.

DOCUMENT

McKinley's "War" Message to Congress

McKinley's message of April 11, 1898, attempted to summarize American relations with Cuba. Read it carefully to gain an understanding of his perception of events.

Obedient to that precept of the Constitution which commands the President to give from time to time to the Congress information of the state of the Union and to recommend to their consideration such measures as he shall judge necessary and expedient, it becomes my duty now to address your body with regard to the grave crisis that has arisen in the relations of the United States to Spain by reason of the warfare that for more than three years has raged in the neighboring island of Cuba. . . .

Since the present revolution began, in February, 1895, this country has seen the fertile domain at our threshold ravaged by fire and sword in the course of a struggle unequaled in the history of the island and rarely paralleled as to the numbers of the combatants and the bitterness of the contest by any revolution of modern times where a dependent people striving to be free have been opposed by the power of the sovereign state. . . .

Our trade has suffered, the capital invested by our citizens in Cuba has been largely lost, and the temper and forbearance of our people have been so sorely tried as to beget a perilous unrest among our own citizens. . . .

The agricultural population to the estimated number of 300,000 or more was herded within the towns and their immediate vicinage, deprived of the means of support, rendered destitute of shelter, left poorly clad, and exposed to the most unsanitary conditions. As the scarcity of food increased with the devastation of the depopulated areas of production, destitution and want became misery and starvation. Month by month the death rate increased in an alarming ratio. By March, 1897, according to conservative estimates from official Spanish sources, the mortality among the reconcentrados from starvation and diseases thereto incident exceeded 50 per cent of their total number. . . .

The war in Cuba is of such a nature that short of subjugation or extermination, a final military victory for either side seems impracticable. The alternative lies in the physical exhaustion of the one or the other party, or perhaps of both. . . . The prospect of such a protraction and conclusion of the present strife is a contingency hardly to be contemplated with equanimity by the civilized world, and least of all by the United States, affected and injured as we are, deeply and intimately, by its very existence. . . .

The forcible intervention of the United States as a neutral to stop the war, according to the large dictates of humanity and following many historical precedents where neighboring States have interfered to check the hopeless sacrifices of life by internecine conflicts beyond their borders, is justifiable on rational grounds. It involves, however, hostile constraint upon both the parties to the contest as well to enforce a truce as to guide the eventual settlement.

. . . The present condition of affairs in Cuba is a constant menace to our peace and entails upon this Government an enormous expense. With such a conflict waged for years in an island so near us and with which our people have such trade and business relations; when the lives and liberty of our citizens are in constant danger and their property destroyed and themselves ruined; where our trading vessels are liable to seizure and are seized at our very door by war ships of a foreign nation, the expeditions of filibustering that we are powerless to prevent altogether, and the irritating questions and entanglements thus arising—all these and others that I need not mention, with the resulting strained relations, are a constant menace to our peace and compel us to keep on a semi-war footing with a nation with which we are at peace.

These elements of danger and disorder already pointed out have been strikingly illustrated by a tragic event which has deeply and justly moved the American people. I have already transmitted to Congress the report of the naval court of inquiry on the destruction of the battle ship *Maine* in the harbor of Havana during the night of the 15th of February. The destruction of that noble vessel has filled the national heart with inexpressible horror. Two hundred and fifty-eight brave sailors and marines and two officers of our Navy, reposing in the fancied security of a friendly harbor, have been hurled to death, grief and want brought to their homes and sorrow to the nation.

The naval court of inquiry, which, it is needless to say, commands the unqualified confidence of the Government, was unanimous in its conclusion that the destruction of the *Maine* was caused by an exterior explosion—that of a submarine mine. It did not assume to place the responsibility. That remains to be fixed.

In any event the destruction of the *Maine,* by whatever exterior cause, is a patent and impressive proof of a state of things in Cuba that is intolerable. That condition is thus shown to be such that the Spanish Government can not assure safety and security to a vessel of the American Navy in the harbor of Havana on a mission of peace, and rightfully there.

In view of these facts and of these considerations I ask the Congress to authorize and empower the President to take measures to secure a full and final termination of hostilities between the Government of Spain and the people of Cuba, and to secure in the island the establishment of a stable government, capable of maintaining order and observing its international obligations, insuring peace and tranquillity and the security of its citizens as well as our own, and to use the military and naval forces of the United States as may be necessary for these purposes. . . .

The issue is now with the Congress. It is a solemn responsibility. I have exhausted every effort to relieve the intolerable condition of affairs which is at our doors. . . .

Yesterday, and since the preparation of the foregoing message, official information was received by me that the latest decree of the Queen Regent of Spain directs General Blanco, in order to prepare and facilitate peace, to proclaim a suspension of hostilities, the duration and details of which have not yet been communicated to me.

This fact with every other pertinent consideration will, I am sure, have your just and careful attention in the solemn deliberations upon which you are about to enter. If this measure attains a successful result, then our aspirations as a Christian, peace-loving people will be realized. If it fails, it will be only another justification for our contemplated action.

[James D. Richardson (ed.), *A Compilation of the Messages and Papers of the Presidents, 1789–1897* (Washington, D.C.: U.S. Government Printing Office, 1899), 10: 139–150]

Questions for Reflection

Does McKinley anywhere in the message ask Congress to declare war on Spain? How could a declaration of war be justified in light of his request? How accurate was McKinley's description of developments between Cuba and the United States? Can you see any reason why Congress might have been skeptical of McKinley's claim that Spain had offered to cease hostilities in Cuba? Does this document suggest that the United States was justified in becoming involved in the Cuban matter and ultimately in the Spanish-American War?

ANSWERS TO MULTIPLE-CHOICE AND TRUE-FALSE QUESTIONS

Multiple-Choice Questions

1-A, 2-B, 3-D, 4-D, 5-A, 6-C, 7-B, 8-D

True-False Questions

1-T, 2-F, 3-F, 4-F, 5-F, 6-F, 7-F, 8-T

23

PROGRESSIVISM:
ROOSEVELT, TAFT, AND WILSON

CHAPTER OBJECTIVES

After you complete the reading and study of this chapter you should be able to

1. Explain the nature and the goals of the progressive movement.
2. Compare the progressive movement with the populist movement.
3. Describe Roosevelt's brand of progressivism.
4. Account for Taft's mixed record as a progressive.
5. Describe Wilson's efforts for progressive reform.
6. Assess the impact of progressivism on American politics, society, and economy.

CHAPTER OUTLINE

I. The nature of progressivism
   A. General features
     1. Aimed against the abuses of the Gilded Age bosses
     2. More businesslike and efficient than populism
     3. A paradox of regulation of business by businessmen
     4. A diverse movement

   B. Antecedents
     1. Populism
     2. Mugwumps
     3. Socialist critiques of living and working conditions
     4. Role of the muckrakers
       a. Henry Demarest Lloyd and Lincoln Steffens
       b. Brought about popular support for reform
       c. Stronger on diagnosis than remedy
   C. The themes of progressivism
     1. Efforts to democratize government
       a. Direct primaries
       b. Initiative, referendum, recall, and other local actions
       c. Direct election of senators
     2. A focus on efficiency and good government
       a. Role of Frederick W. Taylor and scientific management
       b. Commission and city-manager forms of city government
       c. Use of specialists in government and business
         i. Robert M. LaFollette
         ii. "Wisconsin Idea"
     3. Regulation of giant corporations
       a. Acceptance and regulation of big business

b. Problem of regulating the
   regulators
4. Impulse toward social justice
   a. Use of private charities and state
      power
   b. Outlawing child labor
   c. Erratic course of the Supreme
      Court
   d. Restricting working hours and
      dangerous occupations
   e. Stricter building codes and
      factory inspection acts
   f. Pressure for prohibition

II. Roosevelt's progressivism
   A. Need for his cautious role
   B. Focus on trust regulation
      1. Opposition to wholesale
         trust-busting
      2. Northern Securities case (1904)
         used to promote the issue
   C. Coal strike of 1902
      1. Basis for the UMW strike
      2. Recalcitrant attitude of
         management
      3. Roosevelt's efforts to force
         arbitration
      4. Effects of the incident
   D. Congressional action
      1. Department of Commerce and
         Labor
      2. Elkins Act
   E. Other antitrust suits

III. TR's second term
   A. Election of 1904
      1. Republican nomination
      2. Democratic positions and
         candidate
      3. Campaign and results
   B. Roosevelt's legislative leadership
      1. Hepburn Act
      2. Roosevelt's support of regulation of
         food and drugs
         a. Role of muckrakers: Upton
            Sinclair and others
         b. Legislation achieved
   C. Efforts for conservation
      1. Earlier movements for
         conservation
      2. Roosevelt's actions

IV. Taft's administration
   A. Selection of a successor in 1908
      1. TR's choice

2. Democrats and Bryan
3. Election results
   B. Taft's background and character
   C. Campaign for tariff reform
      1. Problems in the Senate
      2. Taft's clash with the Progressive
         Republicans
   D. Ballinger-Pinchot controversy
   E. Roosevelt's response upon his return
      to the United States
      1. Initial silence
      2. Development of the New
         Nationalism
      3. TR enters the race
   F. Taft's achievements

V. The election of 1912
   A. The Republican nomination of 1912
   B. Creation of the Progressive party
   C. Wilson's rise to power
      1. His background
      2. His actions in New Jersey
      3. His nomination
   D. Focus of the campaign on the New
      Nationalism and the New Freedom
   E. Wilson's election
   F. Significance of the election of 1912
      1. High-water mark for progressivism
      2. Brought Democrats back into office
      3. Brought southerners into control

VI. Wilsonian reform
   A. Wilson's style
   B. Tariff reform
      1. Personal appearance before
         Congress
      2. Tariff changes in the
         Underwood-Simmons Act
      3. Income tax provisions
   C. The Federal Reserve Act
      1. Compromises required
      2. Description of the Federal Reserve
         System
   D. Efforts for new antitrust laws
      1. Wilson's approach in 1912
      2. Federal Trade Commission Act
         (September 1914)
      3. Clayton Antitrust Act (October
         1914)
         a. Practices outlawed
         b. Provisions for labor and farm
            organizations
      4. Disappointments with
         administration of the new laws

E. The shortcomings of Wilson's progressivism
F. Wilson's return to reform
  1. Plight of the Progressive party
  2. Appointment of Brandeis to the Supreme Court
  3. Support for land banks and long-term farm loans
  4. Farm demonstration agents and agricultural education
  5. Labor reform legislation
VII. The paradoxes of progressivism
  A. Disfranchisement of southern blacks
  B. Manipulation of democratic reforms
  C. Decision making by faceless bureaucratic experts
  D. Decline of voter participation
  E. From optimism to war

KEY ITEMS OF CHRONOLOGY

Roosevelt administration	1901–1909
Anthracite coal strike	1902
Northern Securities Case	1904
Elkins Act	1903
Hepburn Act	1906
Pure Food and Drug Act	1906
Wilson administrations	1913–1921
Sixteenth Amendment (income tax) ratified	1913
Seventeenth Amendment (direct Senate election) ratified	1913
Underwood-Simmons Tariff Act	1913
Federal Reserve Act	1913
Federal Trade Commission Act	1914
Clayton Antitrust Act	1914
Adamson Act	1916

TERMS TO MASTER

Listed below are some important terms or people with which you should be familiar after you complete the study of this chapter. Explain the significance of each name or term.

1. muckrakers
2. initiative and referendum
3. Frederick W. Taylor
4. Northern Securities case
5. anthracite coal strike
6. Robert M. La Follette
7. Elkins Act
8. Hepburn Act
9. Upton Sinclair's *The Jungle*
10. Ballinger-Pinchot controversy
11. New Nationalism
12. New Freedom
13. Federal Reserve System
14. Federal Trade Commission
15. Clayton Antitrust Act

VOCABULARY BUILDING

Listed below are some words used in this chapter. Look up each word in your dictionary.

1. antecedent
2. foster
3. salient
4. dissolution
5. intrastate
6. dubious
7. arbitration
8. irrevocably

EXERCISES FOR UNDERSTANDING

When you have completed reading the chapter, answer each of the following questions. If you have difficulty, go back and reread the section of the chapter related to the question.

Multiple-Choice Questions

Select the letter of the response that best completes the statement.

1. Antecedents contributing to the rise of progressivism included all of the following *except*
   A. Mugwump reformers.
   B. populism.
   C. isolationism.
   D. socialism.

2. Social justice reforms included
   A. laws restricting child labor.
   B. the Sherman Antitrust Act.
   C. the initiative and the referendum.
   D. the Seventeenth Amendment to the Constitution.

3. In dealing with trusts, President Roosevelt
   A. tried to restore small businesses.
   B. wanted efficient regulation.
   C. was a powerful trust-buster.
   D. advocated government ownership of large industry.

4. Under President Roosevelt, Gifford Pinchot directed programs related to the
   A. breaking up of trusts.
   B. conservation of natural resources.
   C. protection of consumers of foods and drugs.
   D. regulation of the major railroads.

5. In the Ballinger-Pinchot controversy, President Taft
   A. stayed out and let the courts settle it.
   B. followed the policy established by Roosevelt.
   C. fired Ballinger for insubordination.
   D. did none of the above.

6. The phrase "Hamiltonian means to achieve Jeffersonian ends" summarizes the 1912 views of
   A. Woodrow Wilson.
   B. William Howard Taft.
   C. Theodore Roosevelt.
   D. Eugene V. Debs.

7. The Clayton Antitrust Act attempted to regulate trusts by
   A. defining actions of unfair competition.
   B. placing control in a small group of regulators.
   C. taking control of trusts from the courts.
   D. repealing the Sherman Antitrust Act.

8. About 1916, Wilson renewed his support for progressive reforms because
   A. he needed to build a coalition for reelection.
   B. World War I gave the president unlimited powers to act.
   C. he was about to leave office and wanted to create an enduring legacy.
   D. all of the above are true

True-False Questions

Indicate whether each statement is true or false.

1. Muckraker Henry Demarest Lloyd exposed the evils of the Standard Oil Company.

2. The easiest problem for progressives to solve was the regulation of business.

3. In the anthracite coal strike of 1902 President Roosevelt used troops to keep the mines open.

4. Taft brought more antitrust suits in four years than TR did in eight years.

5. Robert La Follette ran for president on the Progressive party ticket in 1912.

6. Before entering politics Woodrow Wilson worked as president of a large industrial corporation.

7. The Underwood-Simmons Tariff of 1913 sought to restore competition by lowering import duties.

8. Wilson preferred the Federal Trade Commission Act to the Clayton Antitrust Act.

Essay Questions

1. Explain the major themes of progressivism.
2. Explain the significance of the election of 1912.
3. Compare and contrast the policies of Presidents Roosevelt and Wilson regarding big business.
4. In what ways was President Taft a progressive?
5. Was Theodore Roosevelt or Wilson the more successful progressive president? Explain your answer.
6. What were the limitations of progressivism? What lasting contributions did it make?

DOCUMENT

Wilson's First Inaugural Address, March 4, 1913

Woodrow Wilson's first inaugural address is an eloquent expression of the New Freedom philosophy he espoused during the 1912 campaign. Reprinted here in its entirety, the address also set the legislative agenda for Wilson's first term.

My Fellow Citizens:

There has been a change of government. It began two years ago, when the House of Representatives became Democratic by a decisive majority. It has now been completed. The Senate about to assemble will also be Democratic. The offices of President and Vice-President have been put into the hands of Democrats. What does the change mean? That is the question that is uppermost in our minds to-day. That is the question I am going to try to answer, in order, if I may, to interpret the occasion.

It means much more than the mere success of a party. The success of a party means little except when the Nation is using that party for a large and definite purpose. No one can mistake the purpose for which the Nation now seeks to use the Democratic Party. It seeks to use it to interpret a change in its own plans and point of view. Some old things with which we had grown familiar, and which had begun to creep into the very habit of our thought and of our lives, have altered their aspect as we have latterly looked critically upon them, with fresh, awakened eyes; have dropped their disguises and shown themselves alien and sinister. Some new things, as we look frankly upon them, willing to comprehend their real character, have come to assume the aspect of things long believed in and familiar, stuff of our own convictions. We have been refreshed by a new insight into our own life.

We see that in many things that life is very great. It is incomparably great in its material aspects, in its body of wealth, in the diversity and sweep of its energy, in the industries which have been conceived and built up by the genius of individual men and the limitless enterprise of groups of men. It is great, also, very great, in its moral force.

Nowhere else in the world have noble men and women exhibited in more striking forms the beauty and the energy of sympathy and helpfulness and counsel in their efforts to rectify wrong, alleviate suffering, and set the weak in the way of strength and hope. We have built up, moreover, a great system of government, which has stood through a long age as in many respects a model for those who seek to set liberty upon foundations that will endure against fortuitous change, against storm and accident. Our life contains every great thing, and contains it in rich abundance.

But the evil has come with the good, and much fine gold has been corroded. With riches has come inexcusable waste. We have squandered a great part of what we might have used, and have not stopped to conserve the exceeding bounty of nature, without which our genius for enterprise would have been worthless and impotent, scorning to be careful, shamefully prodigal as well as admirably efficient. We have been proud of our industrial achievements, but we have not hitherto stopped thoughtfully enough to count the human cost, the cost of lives snuffed out, of energies overtaxed and broken, the fearful physical and spiritual cost to the men and women and children upon whom the dead weight and burden of it all has fallen pitilessly the years through. The groans and agony of it all had not yet reached our ears, the solemn, moving undertone of our life, coming up out of the mines and factories and out of every home where the struggle had its initimate and familiar seat. With the great Government went many deep secret things which we too long delayed to look into and scrutinize with candid, fearless eyes. The great Government we loved has too often been made use of for private and selfish purposes, and those who used it had forgotten the people.

At last a vision has been vouchsafed us of our life as a whole. We see the bad with the good, the debased and decadent with the sound and vital. With this vision we approach new affairs. Our duty is to cleanse, to reconsider, to restore, to correct the evil without impairing the good, to purify and humanize every process of our common life without weakening or sentimentalizing it. There has been something crude and heartless and unfeeling in our haste to succeed and be great. Our thought has been "Let every man look out for himself, let every generation look out for itself," while we reared giant machinery which made it impossible that any but those who stood at the levers of control should have a chance to look out for themselves. We had not forgotten our morals. We remembered well enough that we had set up a policy which was meant to serve the humblest as well as the most powerful, with an eye single to the standards of justice and fair play, and remembered it with pride. But we were very heedless and in a hurry to be great.

We have come now to the sober second thought. The scales of heedlessness have fallen from our eyes. We have made up our minds to square every process of our national life again with the standards we so proudly set up at the beginning and have always carried at our hearts. Our work is a work of restoration.

We have itemized with some degree of particularity the things that ought to be altered and here are some of the chief items: A tariff which cuts us off from our proper part in the commerce of the world, violates the just principles of taxation, and makes the Government a facile instrument in the hands of private interests; a banking and currency system based upon the necessity of the Government to sell its bonds fifty years ago and perfectly adapted to concentrating cash and restricting credits; an industrial system which, take it on all its sides, financial as well as administrative, holds capital in leading strings, restricts the liberties and limits the opportunities of labor, and exploits without renewing or conserving the natural resources of the country; a body of agricultural activities never yet given the efficiency of great business undertakings or served as it should be through the instrumentality of science taken directly to the farm, or afforded the facilities of credit best suited to its practical needs; water-courses undeveloped, waste places unreclaimed, forests untended, fast disappearing without plan or prospect of renewal, unregarded waste heaps at every mine. We have studied as perhaps no other nation has the most effective means of production, but we have not studied cost or economy as we should either as organizers of industry, as statesmen, or as individuals.

Nor have we studied and perfected the means by which government may be put at the service of humanity, in safeguarding the health of the Nation, the health of its men and its women and its children, as well as their rights in the struggle for existence. This is no sentimental duty. The firm basis of government is justice, not pity. These are matters of justice. There can be no equality or opportunity, the first essential of justice in the body politic, if men and women and children be not shielded in their lives, their very vitality, from the consequences of great industrial and social processes which they can not alter, control, or singly cope with. Society must see to it that it does not itself crush or weaken or damage its own constituent parts. The first duty of law is to keep sound the society it serves. Sanitary laws, pure food laws, and laws determining conditions of labor which individuals are powerless to determine for themselves are intimate parts of the very business of justice and legal or efficiency.

These are some of the things we ought to do, and not leave the others undone, the old-fashioned, never-to-be-neglected, fundamental safeguarding of property and of individual right. This is the high enterprise of the new day: To lift everything that concerns our life as a Nation to the light that shines from the hearthfire of every man's conscience and vision of the right. It is inconceivable that we should do this as partisans; it is inconceivable we should do it in ignorance of the facts as they are or in blind haste. We shall restore, not destroy. We shall deal with our economic system as it is and as it may be modified, not as it might be if we had a clean sheet of paper to write upon; and step by step we shall make it what it should be, in the spirit of those who question their own wisdom and seek counsel and knowledge, not shallow self-satisfaction or the excitement of excursions whither they can not tell. Justice, and only justice, shall always be our motto.

And yet it will be no cool process of mere science. The Nation has been deeply stirred, stirred by a solemn passion, stirred by the knowledge of wrong, of ideals lost, of government too often debauched and made an instrument of evil. The feelings with which we face this new age of right and opportunity sweep across our heartstrings like some air out of God's own presence, where justice and mercy are reconciled and the judge and the brother are one. We know our task to be no mere task of politics but a task which shall search us through and through, whether we be able to understand our time and the need of our people, whether we be indeed their spokesmen and interpreters, whether we have the pure heart to comprehend and the rectified will to choose our high course of action.

This is not a day of triumph; it is a day of dedication. Here muster, not the forces of party, but the forces of humanity. Men's hearts wait upon us; men's lives hang in the balance; men's hopes call upon us to say what we will do. Who shall live up to the great trust? Who dares fail to try? I summon all honest men, all patriotic, all forward-looking men, to my side. God helping me, I will not fail them, if they will but counsel and sustain me!

[U.S., 63rd Congress, Special Session, *Senate Doc. 3*]

Questions for Reflection

Why does Wilson begin his address by commenting on the significance of parties? What is Wilson's assessment of American society—its achievements and its failures?

How successful was Wilson in implementing his legislative goals? Was he effective in changing "the things that ought to be altered"?

ANSWERS TO MULTIPLE-CHOICE AND TRUE-FALSE QUESTIONS

Multiple-Choice Questions

1-C, 2-A, 3-B, 4-B, 5-D, 6-C, 7-A, 8-A

True-False Questions

1-T, 2-F, 3-F, 4-T, 5-F, 6-F, 7-T, 8-T

24

WILSON AND THE GREAT WAR

CHAPTER OBJECTIVES

After you complete the reading and study of this chapter you should be able to

1. Describe Wilson's idealistic diplomacy and show the clash of ideals and reality in Mexico.
2. Explain early United States reaction to the World War.
3. Account for the entry of the United States into World War I.
4. Explain the status of civil liberties during World War I and during the Red Scare afterward.
5. Explain the process and product of peacemaking after World War I.
6. Account for the failure of the United States to ratify the peace treaty after World War I.
7. Describe the problems of reconversion from World War I to civilian life.

CHAPTER OUTLINE

I. Wilson and foreign affairs
   A. Inexperience and idealism
   B. Intervention in Mexico
      1. Diaz overthrown in revolution
      2. Nonrecognition of the Huerta government
      3. Invasion at Vera Cruz
      4. Carranza's government
      5. The pursuit of Pancho Villa
   C. Problems in the Caribbean

II. World War I and the early American response
   A. Outbreak of the war
   B. Initial American response
      1. Declaration of neutrality
      2. Attitudes of hyphenated Americans
      3. Views of other American groups
      4. Effect of propaganda on Americans
   C. Extension of economic credit to the Allies
   D. Problems of neutrality
      1. Conflicts over neutral rights at sea
      2. British declaration of the North Sea war zone and other restrictions
      3. German use of submarines
      4. Sinking of the *Lusitania*
         a. American protests
         b. Bryan's resignation
         c. *Arabic* pledge
   E. Debate over preparedness
      1. Demands for stronger army and navy
      2. Antiwar advocates
      3. National Defense Act of 1916
      4. Move for a stronger navy
      5. Efforts to obtain revenue for preparedness

III. Election of 1916
   A. Republicans nominated

B. Democratic program
C. Issues of the campaign
D. Results of the election

IV. Steps toward war
   A. Wilson's effort to mediate
   B. Wilson's assertion of terms of peace
   C. German decision for unrestricted submarine warfare
   D. Diplomatic break with Germany
   E. The Zimmerman telegram
   F. The Russian Revolution

V. United States's entry into the war
   A. The sinking of American vessels
   B. Wilson's call for war
   C. An assessment of reasons for United States's entry into the war
   D. Limited expectations from the U.S.
   E. Financial assistance to the Allies
   F. First contingents of troops

VI. Mobilizing a nation
   A. Raising the armed forces
   B. Regulation of the economy
   C. War Industries Board
   D. Changes in labor
      a. Blacks
      b. Mexican-Americans
      c. Women
      d. Unions
   E. Committee on Public Information
   F. Civil liberties in the war
      1. Popular disdain for all things German
      2. Espionage and Sedition Acts
         a. Terms of the acts
         b. Prosecutions
         c. Impact of the acts
         d. *Schenck v. United States*

VII. The American role in war
   A. Little action through 1917
   B. American offensives in 1918
   C. The Fourteen Points
      1. Origins

2. Content
3. Purposes
4. Responses
D. Terms of the armistice
E. Intervention in Russia

VIII. The fight for the peace
   A. Wilson's role
      1. Decision to attend the peace conference
      2. Effects of congressional elections of 1918
      3. Wilson's reception in Europe
      4. Structure of the conference
   B. Emphasis on the League of Nations
      1. Article X of the charter
      2. Machinery of the League
   C. Early warning from Lodge
   D. Amendments made to respond to critics at home
   E. Compromises on national self-determination
   F. The agreement for reparations
   G. Obtaining the German signature

IX. Wilson's loss at home
   A. Support for the peace
   B. Lodge's reaction
   C. Opponents of the treaty
   D. Wilson's speaking tour
   E. Wilson's stroke
   F. Failure of the Senate votes
   G. Formal ending of the war

X. Conversion to peace
   A. Spanish flu epidemic
   B. Lack of leadership and planning
   C. Postwar boom and slump
   D. Labor unrest
   E. Race riots
   F. The Red Scare
      1. Fear of radicals
      2. Bombs in the mail
      3. Deportation of aliens
      4. Evaporation of the Red Scare
      5. Legacy of the Red Scare

KEY ITEMS OF CHRONOLOGY

Huerta in power in Mexico	February 1913
Invasion of Vera Cruz	April 1914
Outbreak of World War I	August 1914
Lusitania sunk	May 1915

Arabic pledge from Germany	September 1915
Germany resumed unrestricted submarine warfare	February 1917
United States declared war	April 1917
Creation of War Industries Board	July 1917
Armistice	November 1918
Paris Peace Conference	January-May 1919
Senate votes on treaty	November 1919 and March 1920
Red Scare	1919–1920

TERMS TO MASTER

Listed below are some important terms or people with which you should be familiar after you complete the study of this chapter. Explain the significance of each name or term.

1. Victoriano Huerta
2. hyphenated Americans
3. Central Powers
4. *Lusitania*
5. *Arabic* pledge
6. Revenue Act of 1916
7. Zimmerman telegram
8. War Industries Board
9. Committee on Public Information
10. Espionage and Sedition Acts
11. *Schenck v. United States*
12. Fourteen Points
13. Big Four
14. Henry Cabot Lodge
15. reparations
16. Irreconcilables
17. Boston Police Strike
18. A. Mitchell Palmer
19. Red Scare

VOCABULARY BUILDING

Listed below are some words used in this chapter. Look up each word in your dictionary.

1. obliquely
2. enmity
3. autocracy
4. attrition
5. magnanimous
6. ruse
7. bellicosity
8. envoy
9. conscription
10. peevish
11. virulent

EXERCISES FOR UNDERSTANDING

When you have completed the reading of the chapter, answer each of the following questions. If you have difficulty, go back and reread the section of the chapter related to the question.

Multiple-Choice Questions

Select the letter of the response that best completes the statement.

1. When World War I began in Europe,
   A. most Americans supported Germany.
   B. Irish-Americans and German-Americans instinctively opposed the Central Powers.
   C. many high U.S. officials were pro-British.
   D. none of the above was true

2. After the sinking of the *Lusitania*, William Jennings Bryan
   A. urged Wilson to declare war.
   B. resigned in protest over American demands on Germany.
   C. called for arming all passenger ships.
   D. campaigned for strengthening the military preparation for war.

3. The Revenue Act of 1916 placed most of the financial burden of preparedness on
   A. the farmers.
   B. munitions manufacturers.
   C. banks that lent money to foreign nations.
   D. wealthy persons.

4. The Zimmerman telegram
   A. asked Theodore Roosevelt to raise an army battalion to go to war.
   B. revealed Germany's policy of unrestricted submarine warfare.
   C. warned Germany not to sink unarmed passenger ships.
   D. suggested a wartime alliance between Mexico and Germany.

5. The wartime Espionage and Sedition Acts
   A. were upheld by the Supreme Court.
   B. led to the persecution of more than 1,500 people.
   C. hit hard at socialists and radicals.
   D. did all the above

6. The U.S. sent troops into Russia in 1918 to
   A. support the Bolshevik revolution.
   B. maintain the fighting against Germany in the East.
   C. protect Allied supplies in Russia.
   D. ensure Russian participation in postwar negotiations.

7. For Wilson the most important part of the peace negotiations involved
   A. the League of Nations.
   B. Germany's admission of "war guilt".
   C. war debts and reparations.
   D. the principle of self-determination.

8. In the U. S., the Spanish flu epidemic
   A. killed 500,000 people.
   B. originated in the Midwest.
   C. hit the elderly especially hard.
   D. all of the above

True-False Questions

Indicate whether each statement is true or false.

1. Under President Wilson, United States military forces never intervened in Mexico.
2. The United States did not enter World War I when it began in Europe.
3. "He kept us out of war" was the 1916 Republican campaign cry against Wilson.
4. The War Industries Board was the most important agency mobilizing the nation for war.
5. The Committee on Public Information enforced censorship of newspapers and magazines.
6. With the Fourteen Points, Wilson sought to keep Russia in the war and to create disunity among the Central Powers.
7. Senator Henry Cabot Lodge was a supporter of the Versailles Treaty.
8. The Red Scare was directed against racist and conservative groups like the KKK.

Essay Questions

1. Was Wilson's policy toward Mexico characteristic of his diplomacy? Explain.
2. Trace the major developments in American policy on intervention from the start of World War I in 1914 to the United States entry into the War in 1917.
3. Describe the Red Scare that followed World War I. Were restrictions on civil liberties justified in this case? Why or why not?
4. Describe how the United States mobilized men, arms, and money for World War I.
5. What factors led to the defeat of Wilson's plans for the postwar peace? Assess Wilson's success as a leader in foreign policy.
6. Assess the American contribution to the Allied victory in World War I.

DOCUMENT

The Fourteen Points: Wilson's Address to Congress, January 8, 1918

In his famous address to Congress of January 8, 1918, Wilson explained the war aims of the United States. His Fourteen Points formed the basis for peace negotiations.

Gentlemen of the Congress:

. . . It will be our wish and purpose that the processes of peace, when they are begun, shall be absolutely open and that they shall involve and permit henceforth no secret understandings of any kind. The day of conquest and aggrandizement is gone by; so is also the day of secret covenants entered into in the interest of particular governments and likely at some unlooked-for moment to upset the peace of the world. It is this happy fact, now clear to the view of every public man whose thoughts do not still linger in an age that is dead and gone, which makes it possible for every nation whose purposes are consistent with justice and the peace of the world to avow now or at any other time the objects it has in view.

We entered this war because violations of right had occurred which touched us to the quick and made the life of our own people impossible unless they were corrected and the world secured once for all against their recurrence. What we demand in this war, therefore, is nothing peculiar to ourselves. It is that the world be made fit and safe to live in; and particularly that it be made safe for every peace-loving nation which, like our own, wishes to live its own life, determine its own institutions, be assured of justice and fair dealing by the other peoples of the world as against force and selfish aggression. All the peoples of the world are in effect partners in this interest, and for our own part we see very clearly that unless justice be done to others it will not be done to us. The program of the world's peace, therefore, is our program; and that program, the only possible program, as we see it, is this:

I. Open covenants of peace, openly arrived at, after which there shall be no private international understandings of any kind but diplomacy shall proceed always frankly and in the public view.

II. Absolute freedom of navigation upon the seas, outside territorial waters, alike in peace and in war, except as the seas may be closed in whole or in part by international action for the enforcement of international covenants.

III. The removal, so far as possible, of all economic barriers and the establishment of an equality of trade conditions among all the nations consenting to the peace and associating themselves for its maintenance.

IV. Adequate guarantees given and taken that national armaments will be reduced to the lowest point consistent with domestic safety.

V. A free, open-minded, and absolutely impartial adjustment of all colonial claims, based upon a strict observance of the principle that in determining all such questions of sovereignty the interests of the populations concerned must have equal weight with the equitable claims of the government whose title is to be determined.

VI. The evacuation of all Russian territory and such a settlement of all questions affecting Russia as will secure the best and freest coöperation of the other nations of the world in obtaining for her an unhampered and unembarrassed opportunity for the independent determination of her own political development and national policy and assure her of a sincere welcome into the society of free nations under institutions of her own choosing; and, more than a welcome, assistance also of every kind that she may need and may herself desire. The treatment accorded Russia by her sister nations in the months to come will be the acid test of their good will, of their comprehension of her needs as distinguished from their own interests, and of their intelligent and unselfish sympathy.

VII. Belgium, the whole world will agree, must be evacuated and restored, without any attempt to limit the sovereignty which she enjoys in common with all other free nations. No other single act will serve as this will serve to restore confidence among the nations in the laws which they have themselves set and determined for the government of their relations with one another. Without this healing act the whole structure and validity of international law is forever impaired.

VIII. All French territory should be freed and the invaded portions restored, and the wrong done to France by Prussia in 1871 in the matter of Alsace-Lorraine, which has unsettled the peace of the world for nearly fifty years, should be righted, in order that peace may once more be made secure in the interest of all.

IX. A readjustment of the frontiers of Italy should be effected along clearly recognizable lines of nationality.

X. The peoples of Austria-Hungary, whose place among the nations we wish to see safeguarded and assured, should be accorded the freest opportunity of autonomous development.

XI. Rumania, Serbia, and Montenegro should be evacuated; occupied territories restored; Serbia accorded free and secure access to the sea; and the relations of the several Balkan states to one another determined by friendly counsel along historically established lines of allegiance and nationality; and international guarantees of the political and economic independence and territorial integrity of the several Balkan states should be entered into.

XII. The Turkish portions of the present Ottoman Empire should be assured a secure sovereignty, but the other nationalities which are now under Turkish rule should be assured an undoubted security of life and an absolutely unmolested opportunity of autonomous development, and the Dardanelles should be permanently opened as a free passage to the ships and commerce of all nations under international guarantees.

XIII. An independent Polish state should be erected which should include the territories inhabited by indisputably Polish populations, which should be assured a free and secure access to the sea, and whose political and economic independence and territorial integrity should be guaranteed by international covenant.

XIV. A general association of nations must be formed under specific covenants for the purpose of affording mutual guarantees of political independence and territorial integrity to great and small states alike.

In regard to these essential rectifications of wrong and assertions of right we feel ourselves to be intimate partners of all the governments and peoples associated together against the Imperialists. We cannot be separated in interest or divided in purpose. We stand together until the end.

For such arrangements and covenants we are willing to fight and to continue to fight until they are achieved; but only because we wish the right to prevail and desire a just and stable peace such as can be secured only by removing the chief provocations to war, which this program does not remove. We have no jealousy of German greatness, and there is nothing in this program that impairs it. We grudge her no achievement or distinction of learning or of pacific enterprise such as have made her record very bright and very enviable. We do not wish to injure her or to block in any way her legitimate influence or power. We do not wish to fight her either with arms or with hostile arrangements of trade if she is willing to associate herself with us and the other peace-loving nations of the world in covenants of justice and law and fair dealing. We wish her only to accept a place of equality among the peoples of the world,—the new world in which we now live,—instead of a place of mastery.

Neither do we presume to suggest to her any alteration or modification of her institutions. But it is necessary, we must frankly say, and necessary as a preliminary to any intelligent dealings with her on our part, that we should know whom her spokesmen speak for when they speak to us, whether for the Reichstag majority or for the military party and the men whose creed is imperial domination.

We have spoken now, surely, in terms too concrete to admit of any further doubt or question. An evident principle runs through the whole program I have outlined. It is the principle of justice to all peoples and nationalities, and their right to live on equal terms of liberty and safety with one another, whether they be strong or weak. Unless this principle be made its foundation no part of the structure of international justice can stand. The people of the United States could act upon no other principle; and to the vindication of this principle they are ready to devote their lives, their honor, and everything that they possess. The moral climax of this the culminating and final war for human liberty has come, and they are ready to put their own strength, their own highest purpose, their own integrity and devotion to the test.

[From *A Compilation of the Messages and Papers of the Presidents,* Supplement, 1917–1921 (New York: Bureau of National Literature, Inc., 1921), 2: 8421*ff*]

Questions for Reflection

Were Wilson's Fourteen Points a practical program for peace? Explain. Describe the controversy sparked by Point XIV. How would you assess Wilson's role in this controversy? Is the "principle of justice to all peoples and nationalities" a useful basis for foreign policy? Why or why not?

ANSWERS TO MULTIPLE-CHOICE
AND TRUE-FALSE QUESTIONS

Multiple-Choice Questions

1-C, 2-B, 3-D, 4-D, 5-D, 6-C, 7-A, 8-A

True-False Questions

1-F, 2-T, 3-F, 4-T, 5-F, 6-T, 7-F, 8-F

25

SOCIETY AND CULTURE
BETWEEN THE WARS

CHAPTER OBJECTIVES

After you complete the reading and study of this chapter you should be able to

1. Describe and account for the mood of the 1920s.
2. Describe the nativist reaction in the twenties and the revival of the Ku Klux Klan, along with the consequences of these developments.
3. Trace the emergence of fundamentalism and its effects.
4. Account for the experiment in prohibition and its persistence in the face of widespread evasion of the law.
5. Describe and compare the political and social position of women and blacks in the twenties.
6. Explain the scientific basis of the moral relativism of the decade.
7. Describe the literary flowering of the 1920s and 1930s and the contributions of major American novelists and poets of the era.

CHAPTER OUTLINE

I. Reaction in the 1920s
   A. Changing moods
      1. Disillusionment
      2. Defiance against change
   B. Nativism
      1. Sacco and Vanzetti case
      2. Efforts to restrict immigration
   C. Revival of the Ku Klux Klan
   D. Fundamentalism
      1. Emergence of fundamentalism
      2. William Jennings Bryan
      3. Scopes trial
   E. Prohibition
      1. An expression of reforming zeal
      2. Organization for the cause
      3. Crusade for a constitutional amendment
      4. Effectiveness of prohibition
      5. Its link with organized crime
      6. Al Capone

II. Social tensions
   A. A time of cultural conflict
      1. Urban disdain for rural small-town values
      2. Rural fears of cities
   B. The new morality
      1. Emphasis on youth
      2. Obsession with sex
      3. Impact of Freud
      4. Jazz
   C. The women's movement
      1. The work for women's suffrage

a. Alice Paul and new tactics
b. Contributions of Carrie Chapman Catt
c. Passage and ratification of the amendment
d. Effects of women's suffrage
2. Push for an Equal Rights Amendment
3. Women in the workforce
D. The "New Negro"
  1. The "Great Migration" north
    a. Demographics
    b. Impact of the move
  2. The Harlem Renaissance
  3. Marcus Garvey and Negro Nationalism
  4. Development of the NAACP
    a. Emergence of the organization
    b. Role of Du Bois
    c. Strategy
    d. The campaign against lynching
    e. Scottsboro case

III. The culture of modernism
A. Loss of faith in progress
B. Einstein and the Theory of Relativity
C. Impact of relativity and uncertainty
  1. Denial of absolute values
  2. Assertion of relativism in cultures
D. Modernist literature
  1. Chief features
    a. Exploration of the irrational

b. Uncertainty seen as desirable
c. Positive view of conflict
d. Formal manners discounted for contact with "reality"
2. Development of artistic bohemias
3. The Armory Show
4. Emphasis on the "new" in many facets of life
5. Role of Harriet Monroe
6. Chief American prophets of modernism
  a. Ezra Pound
  b. T. S. Eliot
  c. Gertrude Stein
7. Expatriates
  a. F. Scott Fitzgerald
  b. Ernest Hemingway
    i. Cult of masculinity
    ii. Terse literary style

IV. Return of social significance
A. Impact of the depression
B. Allegiance to revolution
C. Novels of social significance
  1. John Steinbeck
  2. Richard Wright
D. The Southern Renaissance
  1. Effect of Mencken's critique of the South
  2. Novelists of note
    a. Thomas Wolfe
    b. William Faulkner
E. The rediscovery of American culture

KEY ITEMS OF CHRONOLOGY

Einstein's paper on the Theory of Relativity	1905
Organization of the NAACP	1910
Ratification of the Eighteenth Amendment (prohibition)	1919
Ratification of the Nineteenth Amendment (women's suffrage)	1920
Sinclair Lewis's *Babbitt*	1922
Scopes trial	1924
Hemingway's *The Sun Also Rises*	1926
Execution of Sacco and Vanzetti	1927
Heisenberg's Principle of Uncertainty stated	1927
Scottsboro case	1931
John Steinbeck's *The Grapes of Wrath*	1939
Richard Wright's *Native Son*	1940

TERMS TO MASTER

Listed below are some important terms or people with which you should be familiar after you complete the study of this chapter. Explain the significance of each name or term.

1. Sacco and Vanzetti
2. KKK
3. "monkey trial"
4. Sigmund Freud
5. Eighteenth Amendment
6. "Great Migration"
7. Marcus Garvey
8. NAACP
9. Theory of Relativity
10. modernist movement
11. F. Scott Fitzgerald
12. Ernest Hemingway
13. John Steinbeck
14. Richard Wright
15. "The Sahara of the Bozart"
16. Thomas Wolfe
17. William Faulkner

VOCABULARY BUILDING

Listed below are some words used in this chapter. Look up each word in your dictionary.

1. sedition
2. nativism
3. visceral
4. anticlimactic
5. prescience
6. banality
7. sublimation
8. ephemeral
9. bohemia
10. expatriates

EXERCISES FOR UNDERSTANDING

When you have completed reading the chapter, answer each of the following questions. If you have difficulty, go back and reread the section of the chapter related to the question.

Multiple-Choice Questions

Select the letter of the response that best completes the statement.

1. In the United States, the end of World War I brought
   A. a renewed belief in the old values of glory, honor, and courage.
   B. the optimistic conviction that the world was constantly improving.
   C. disillusionment with modern civilization.
   D. a greater appreciation of diversity and change in American life.

2. Obstacles to prohibition included
   A. profits from bootlegging.
   B. inadequate congressional support for enforcement.
   C. public demand for alcohol.
   D. all of the above

3. The immigration acts of the 1920s were designed to
   A. reduce immigration from all countries except England.
   B. allow immigration only from Latin America.
   C. reduce immigration from southern and eastern Europe.
   D. increase immigration from England and Germany.

4. The ideas of Sigmund Freud affected American attitudes about
   A. the Scopes trial in 1924.
   B. sex and morality.
   C. efforts to start a Negro republic in Africa.
   D. the importance of quanta.

5. The Harlem Renaissance, an artistic and literary blossoming, featured the works of
   A. Claude McKay, Langston Hughes, and Countee Cullen.
   B. H. L. Mencken, Eugene O'Neill, and Sinclair Lewis.
   C. Thomas Wolfe, Ernest Hemingway, and the Fugitives.
   D. Albert Einstein, Sigmund Freud, and Marcus Garvey.

6. The scientific work of Einstein, Heisenberg, and others

A. reinforced the traditional faith in reason and order.
B. increased confidence in man's ability to fully understand the world.
C. was incompatible with the disillusionment and despair of the postwar period.
D. suggested that there is a limit to man's understanding of the universe.

7. The features of modernist literature included *all but which one* of the following:
A. exploration of the irrational as an essential part of human nature.
B. the view of the universe as operating on unchanging and stable principles.
C. the view that conflict was more fundamental than harmony.
D. the view that freedom from convention was more important than following tradition.

8. John Steinbeck's *The Grapes of Wrath* is a novel reflecting
A. modernist writing.
B. the Harlem Renaissance.
C. social concerns in the depression.
D. the Southern Renaissance.

True-False Questions

Indicate whether each statement is true or false.

1. The Ku Klux Klan was directed against blacks, Jews, and Catholics.
2. John T. Scopes's conviction for a payroll robbery and murder in Indiana led to the downfall of the KKK.

3. Organized crime began during the depression.
4. The Nineteenth Amendment to the Constitution gave women the right to vote.
5. The NAACP's strategy stressed working through the legal system to achieve changes in race relations.
6. The chief American prophets of modernism in literature lived in Europe.
7. The leading black novelist during the depression was Richard Wright.
8. In varying the usual rhetorical strategies so that new insights would take the reader by surprise, William Faulkner was one of the most skilled modernist writers.

Essay Questions

1. In what ways were the 1920s a time of social and intellectual defensiveness and disillusionment?
2. Describe the "new morality" of the 1920s.
3. Compare and contrast the Harlem Renaissance and the Southern Renaissance.
4. Explain the contributions of Freud, Marx, Einstein, and Heisenberg to the new mood of the twenties.
5. What were the chief features of modernist literature? Show how those features were exhibited in the works of one of the authors mentioned in the text.
6. How did the depression transform the literary outlook of the twenties into that of the thirties?

DOCUMENT

Testimony about the Work of the Ku Klux Klan

These excerpts from testimony before a congressional inquiry give some insight into the work of the Ku Klux Klan in the 1920s.

    Mr. Campbell. Mr. Wright, will you state your name to the stenographer?
    Mr. Wright. C. Anderson Wright. . . . I was formerly a member

of the New York klan, king kleagle, assigned as chief of staff of the invisible planet, Knights of the Air. . . .

Mr. Campbell. What were your instructions with respect to whom you should regulate and how, and how you were to serve the klan or uplift the community?

Mr. Wright. My instructions as a klansman were simply starting in and giving the Jews the dickens in New York. Their idea was this, as preached by Clarke and Hooper in my presence, with several other prospective members whom I brought up, that the Jew patronizes the Jew, if possible: therefore, we as klansmen, the only real 100 per cent Americans, will only patronize klansmen. Now, the idea was this, to simply organize everybody that was of their belief and religious belief into this order and they would practice not only moral clannishness but also practical clannishness; in other words a klansman would be compelled to buy from another klansman if possible. That was how it was explained to us by Hooper. He did not really know much about it at that time; he was simply out for the money he could make out of it, and that was also explained by Clarke. They said, "In New York City here we have all the Jews; they are controlling New York; we will get under here and when we have 10,000 members here, if we do not want a certain man to do a certain thing, if this man receives 10,000 letters or telegrams stating that he should not do this thing, he is not very apt to do it." In other words, if a member of the klan should be brought on trial before a certain judge or jury, if that judge or jury received 10,000 requests from New York to do a certain thing, they would be pretty apt to do it. That was their idea of gaining control of the courts.

Mr. Campbell. What, if anything, were you told about the wearing of the mask, or were you told it was important that you should do that.

Mr. Wright. You only wore the mask, according to imperial instructions, when you were in the klavern or klan, and then only when what they called the aliens or strangers or people to be initiated were present. Of course, in official parades it was up to the exalted cyclops. . . .

Mr. Kreider. What was the object to be accomplished, or what were the duties of the aerial service?

Mr. Wright. I will tell you what my idea is and what the ideas of the flyers of this country were. We saw that the Aero Club of America and other organizations were absolutely going out of existence: they were decaying; and we felt that we should get a fraternal order together of flyers to promote commercial aviation and give the boys a chance to fly. We are all reserve officers, or some of us are, and since we have been out of the Army we have never seen an airplane. If we take our reserve documents and go to a field to fly we are told there are no ships available, and we have to go through a certain medical examination, which is ridiculous, but we can not fly. So we got several together. . . .

Mr. Kreider. Did all the members of this organization, known as the Knights of the Air, have to be members of the Ku-Klux Klan?

Mr. Wright. No, sir, but here is where the hitch came, as decided by Clarke; he said, "No man can become an officer of the Knights of the Air who is not a klansman; we will absolutely control the Knights of the Air through having only klansmen as officers." That was the first thing; and then Clarke decided that the equipment that the klan got should be placed in his name and not in the name of the Knights of the Air, his idea being to absolutely control it with an iron hand. As I say, out there it was talked over for two days what we were going to do, and he was very visionary, and he saw Edward Young Clarke controlling the air in America, without question or belief. . . .

Mr. Kreider. Was this organization to be used later on or at any time to terrorize men?

Mr. Wright. Oh, no. The Knights of the Air was simply started into being with the flyers as something to get us together, and was capitalized by Clarke as a money-making plan; that is all. I afterwards saw letters, after I left Atlanta, being sent out under the name of Mr. Cherry, who was a klansman, and an assistant over in the office, who had never seen an airplane, I think, to all the aero clubs and flyers throughout the country, saying what a great thing the Knights of the Air was; in fact, after I left there, there was nobody that I know of that was a flyer or a reserve officer in the Army. It was simply a case of Clarke's ideas being absolutely so that no man could conscientiously go into it as a reserve officer in the United States Army. There is no question about it. The whole Ku-Klux Klan is simply based on treason against the country, in this way, that they have planned and schemed and would have, if not publicly exposed, gotten control of practically every seat of government through their tremendous voting power. In the State of Texas to-day I venture to say that practically all the smaller cities are absolutely controlled by the klan from the mayor on down. Texas should be the headquarters of the Ku-Klux Klan and not Georgia, because in Georgia they all look upon it more as a joke—the Atlanta people. . . .

Mr. Fess. What is the purpose of the parades we hear about?

Mr. Wright. The parades?

Mr. Fess. Yes; we have had statements about terrorizing.

Mr. Wright. Well, the idea is this, which I can prove and will be very glad to file before the committee, by their own semiofficial organ, the Searchlight—the idea was simply to terrorize people by showing their strength. To cite an instance of that, in Dallas, Tex., they were having trouble there with a certain class of the building trades—I do not know just exactly what it was—and the klan decided they would hold a parade to show their strength. So it seems like it was all arranged with the city authorities and the parade was held in Dallas, and they marched down the street in full regalia, and about the time they appeared the lights were all extinguished, and the next day the people were back at work. This is cited in their semiofficial organ and in the press throughout the country. . . .

Mr. Snell. What induced you to disclose the secrets of the klan?

Mr. Wright. Why did I?

Mr. Snell. Yes, anything special?

Mr. Wright. Yes, sir. My reason was simply this: I have nothing against the mass of klansmen. They go into it in ignorance, and I knew that. My idea was not to expose so much race hatred, which would drive lots of people into the klan. In other words, there are enough narrow-minded people who would be glad enough to join an order against the Jews, Catholics, foreign born, and Negroes; but if you can show a man where he was simply taken in and made a goat of in order to get money out of him by selling all these mystic contrivances and show him how his money went and the men it was making wealthy and the women who was behind the whole thing and show him where the man at the head of the order was not receiving any money or the imperial treasury was not receiving any money, I figures the klansmen should know that and would be glad to know that, whether they had done any violence or anything else. In other words, I think to-day the more the papers preach on the Ku-Klux Klan as preaching racial hatred, the more members they are going to get, because there are so many narrow-minded people who will join, but when you can show them where their money goes and what a fool he is made and the character of the people getting it, then I think the klansmen of the country will realize and wake up to what they have gone into.

[The Ku Klux Klan, Committee on Rules, House of Representatives, 67th Cong., 1st sess., pp. 15–27, quoted in *Looking for America*, edited by Stanley I. Kutler (New York: W. W. Norton, 1979), 2: 352–356]

Questions for Reflection

Why does Wright say that the Klan was engaged in treason? What were the prospects for the Klan's success? How did the conditions of America in the twenties help to develop the Klan's attitudes as shown in this document?

ANSWERS TO MULTIPLE-CHOICE AND TRUE-FALSE QUESTIONS

Multiple-Choice Questions

1-C, 2-D, 3-C, 4-A, 5-B, 6-D, 7-B, 8-C

True-False Questions

1-T, 2-F, 3-F, 4-T, 5-T, 6-T, 7-T, 8-T

26

REPUBLICAN RESURGENCE
AND DECLINE, 1920–1932

CHAPTER OBJECTIVES

After you complete the reading and study of this chapter you should be able to

1. Describe the effects of the Harding presidency upon the nation.
2. Explain the new prosperity of the twenties.
3. Describe the features of the economy in the New Era decade.
4. Explain Hoover's policies for the nation and indicate their effects.
5. Account for the stock market crash of 1929.
6. Describe the status of farmers during the twenties.
7. Describe the status of labor unions during the 1920s.

CHAPTER OUTLINE

I. The fate of progressivism in the twenties
  A. Causes for the dissolution of the progressive coalition in Congress
    1. Disaffection with the war and the war's aftermath
    2. Administration and labor
    3. Farmers' concerns
    4. Intellectuals' disillusionment

    5. Middle class preoccupation with business
  B. Survivals of progressivism in the twenties
    1. Domination of Congress
    2. Strong pressure at local levels for "good government" and public services
    3. Reform impulse transformed into the drive for moral righteousness

II. The election of 1920
  A. Mood of the country
  B. Republican shift to the right
  C. Democratic nomination
  D. Results

III. The Harding administration
  A. The Harding appointments
  B. Nature of the Harding presidency
  C. Efforts for economy
    1. Tax cuts
    2. Spending cuts
    3. Tariffs
  D. Deemphasis on regulating agencies
  E. Corruption in the administration
    1. Veterans Bureau
    2. Harry Daugherty
    3. Teapot Dome
    4. Role of Harding
  F. Harding's death
  G. Assessment

IV. The Coolidge years
  A. Character of the man
  B. The election of 1924
    1. Coolidge's control of the Republican party
    2. Dissension among the Democrats
    3. Emergence of the Progressive party
    4. Results of the election
  C. Aspects of the New Era
    1. The consumption ethic
    2. Growth of advertising
    3. Development of the movies
    4. Growth of radio
    5. Aviation
      a. Growth of industry
      b. Charles Lindbergh, Jr.
      c. Amelia Earhart
    6. Impact of the automobile
  D. Hoover's role in the economy
    1. His concept of voluntary cooperation
    2. Growth of the Commerce Department
    3. Promotion of trade associations
    4. The acquiescence of the Supreme Court
  E. Problems in agriculture
    1. Reasons for the agricultural slump
    2. Mechanization of farms
    3. New farm organizations
      a. Marketing associations
      b. Formation of the Farm Bloc in Congress
    4. Legislation favorable to agriculture
      a. Early acts
      b. The McNary-Haugen scheme
  F. Setbacks for unions

    1. Earnings in industry
    2. Efforts to forestall unions
V. The Hoover presidency
  A. The election of 1928
    1. The Republican position
    2. The Democratic choice
    3. Issues of the election
    4. Results
  B. The prospects for success
  C. Hoover's general policies
  D. His support for agriculture
    1. Aids for cooperative marketing
    2. Tariff increases
  E. The speculative mania
    1. The Florida real estate bubble
    2. Development of the Great Bull Market
    3. Efforts to curb the market
  F. The crash
    1. Description of the crash
    2. Immediate effects
    3. Causes for the crash
  G. Efforts for recovery
    1. Advocates of laissez-faire
    2. Hoover's exhortations
    3. Public works and credit
    4. Democratic victory in 1930
    5. International complications
  H. Congressional initiatives
    1. The RFC and its role
    2. Help for financial institutions
    3. Plans for relief
  I. Plight of the farmers and veterans
    1. Means of farmer protest
    2. The Bonus Expeditionary Force
  J. Mood of the nation

KEY ITEMS OF CHRONOLOGY

First radio commercial	1922
Death of Harding	1923
Florida real estate collapse	1926
Lindbergh flight	May 1927
McNary-Haugen bills passed Congress	1927, 1928
Stock market crash	October 1929
Smoot-Hawley Tariff	1930
Hoover's moratorium on war-debt payments	1931
Creation of RFC	1932
Attack on the Bonus Expeditionary Force	July 1932

TERMS TO MASTER

Listed below are some important terms or people with which you should be familiar after you complete the study of this chapter. Explain the significance of each name or term.

1. normalcy
2. Andrew Mellon
3. Teapot Dome affair
4. Robert M. La Follette
5. Calvin Coolidge
6. Amelia Earhart
7. Herbert Hoover
8. associationalism
9. marketing cooperatives
10. McNary-Haugen scheme
11. "yellow dog" contract
12. Alfred E. Smith
13. Agricultural Marketing Act
14. margin buying
15. Reconstruction Finance Corporation
16. Federal Home Loan Bank Act
17. Bonus Expeditionary Force

VOCABULARY BUILDING

Listed below are some words used in this chapter. Look up each word in your dictionary.

1. nostrums
2. impropriety
3. exult
4. cornucopia
5. therapeutic
6. trifling
7. parity
8. portentous
9. exacerbate
10. debacle

EXERCISES FOR UNDERSTANDING

When you have completed reading the chapter, answer each of the following questions. If you have difficulty, go back and reread the section of the chapter related to the question.

Multiple-Choice Questions

Select the letter of the response that best completes the statement.

1. The major issue in the 1920 campaign was
   A. the League of Nations.
   B. prohibition.
   C. the Teapot Dome scandal.
   D. none of the above

2. The Teapot Dome scandal involved
   A. kickbacks to the president.
   B. oil leases in Wyoming.
   C. Harding's extramarital affairs.
   D. tariffs on products from the Orient, especially tea.

3. The year 1920 marked the arrival of the first
   A. motion picture.
   B. solo airplane flight over the Atlantic.
   C. talking movie.
   D. regular radio programs.

4. Mass production in the automobile industry was the creation of
   A. Henry Ford.
   B. Walter E. Flanders.
   C. F. W. Taylor.
   D. all of the above (each contributed in part)

5. As secretary of commerce, Herbert Hoover promoted
   A. keen competition among corporations.
   B. standardization of products (tires, bricks, etc.).
   C. a vigorous trustbusting campaign.
   D. federal ownership of the radio and airline industries.

6. The most important proposal in the 1920s to aid farmers was
   A. the "American Plan."
   B. McNary-Haugenism.
   C. the Volstead Act.
   D. the Smoot-Hawley Tariff.

7. In the 1928 election, Alfred E. Smith represented
   A. the supporters of prohibition.
   B. farmers.
   C. conservative business interests.
   D. urban immigrants.

8. Hoover's approach to recovery placed an emphasis on
   A. government construction of housing.
   B. voluntary efforts of the people.
   C. assistance to European trade.
   D. government aid to the unemployed.

True-False Questions

Indicate whether each statement is true or false.

1. Presidents Harding and Coolidge were leading progressives in the 1920s.
2. During the 1920s, government expenditures declined, the national debt decreased, and tax rates dropped.
3. Senator Robert La Follette of Wisconsin was the Democratic opponent of Coolidge in the 1924 election.
4. The first woman to fly around the world was Amelia Earhart.
5. *Real* wages of labor *increased* in the decade of the 1920s.

6. Buying stocks on margin helped restrain speculation in the stock market.
7. Excessively high wages for labor in the 1920s helped cause the stock market crash in 1929.
8. The Reconstruction Finance Corporation assisted farmers, homeowners, and labor unions.

Essay Questions

1. What happened to progressivism in the 1920s?
2. Were the Harding and Coolidge administrations on the whole successful or not? Explain.
3. Which best describes the 1920s: "normalcy" or "the New Era"? Why?
4. What was Hoover's conception of the role of the federal government and how did he apply it in the 1920s?
5. Evaluate the efforts of both Hoover and Congress to revive the American economy in the late 1920s.

DOCUMENT

Hoover's "Philosophy of Rugged Individualism" Speech

Herbert Hoover wound up his successful 1928 campaign for the presidency in New York City on October 22, 1928, with the speech that follows. In it he clearly explains the social philosophy of the Republicans in the 1920s, and of his campaign in particular.

This campaign now draws near a close. The platforms of the two parties defining principles and offering solutions of various national problems have been presented and are being earnestly considered by our people. . . .

In my acceptance speech I endeavored to outline the spirit and ideals by which I would be guided in carrying that platform into administration. Tonight I will not deal with the multitude of issues which have been already well canvassed. I intend rather to discuss some of those more fundamental principles and ideals upon which I believe the government of the United States should be conducted.
. . .

After the war, when the Republican party assumed administration of the country, we were faced with the problem of determination of the very nature of our national life. During one hundred and fifty years we have builded up a form of self-government and a social system which is peculiarly our own. It differs essentially from all others in the world. It is the American system. It is just as definite and positive a political and social system as has ever been developed on earth. It is founded upon a particular conception of self-government in which decentralized local responsibility is the very base. Further than this, it is founded upon the conception that only through ordered liberty, freedom, and equal opportunity to the individual will his initiative and enterprise spur on the march of progress. And in our insistence upon equality of opportunity has our system advanced beyond all the world.

During the war we necessarily turned to the government to solve every difficult economic problem. The government having absorbed every energy of our people for war, there was no other solution. For the preservation of the state the Federal Government became a centralized despotism which undertook unprecedented responsibilities, assumed autocratic powers, and took over the business of citizens. To a large degree we regimented our whole people temporarily into a socialistic state. However justified in time of war, if continued in peace-time it would destroy not only our American system but with it our progress and freedom as well.

When the war closed, the most vital of all issues both in our own country and throughout the world was whether governments should continue their wartime ownership and operation of many instrumentalities of production and distribution. We were challenged with a peace-time choice between the American system of rugged individualism and a European philosophy of diametrically opposed doctrines—doctrines of paternalism and state socialism. The acceptance of these ideas would have meant the destruction of self-government through centralization of government. It would have meant the undermining of the individual initiative and enterprise through which our people have grown to unparalleled greatness.

The Republican Party from the beginning resolutely turned its face away from these ideas and these war practices. . . . When the Republican Party came into full power it went at once resolutely back to our fundamental conception of the state and the rights and responsibilities of the individual. Thereby it restored confidence and hope in the American people, it freed and stimulated enterprise, it restored the government to its position as an umpire instead of a player in the economic game. For these reasons the American people have gone forward in progress while the rest of the world has halted, and some countries have even gone backwards. If anyone will study the causes of retarded recuperation in Europe, he will find much of it due to stifling of private initiative on one hand, and overloading of the government with business on the other.

There has been revived in this campaign, however, a series of proposals which, if adopted, would be a long step toward the abandonment of our American system and a surrender to the destructive operation of governmental conduct of commercial business. Because the country is faced with difficulty and doubt over certain national problems—that is prohibition, farm relief, and electrical power—our opponents propose that we must thrust government a long way into the businesses which give rise to these problems. In effect, they abandon the tenets of their own party and turn to state socialism as a solution for the difficulties presented by all three. It is proposed that we shall change from prohibition to the state purchase and sale of liquor. If their agricultural relief program means anything, it means that the government shall directly or indirectly buy and sell and fix prices of agricultural products. And we are to go into the hydroelectric power business. In other words, we are confronted with a huge program of government in business.

There is, therefore, submitted to the American people a question of fundamental principle. That is: shall we depart from the principles of our American political and economic system, upon which we have advanced beyond all the rest of the world, in order to adopt methods based on principles destructive of its very foundations? And I wish to emphasize the seriousness of these proposals. I wish to make my position clear; for this goes to the very roots of American life and progress. . . .

I do not wish to be misunderstood in this statement. I am defining a general policy. It does not mean that our government is to part with one iota of its national resources without complete protection to the public interest. I have already stated that where the government is engaged in public works for purposes of flood control, of navigation, of irrigation, of scientific research or national defense, or in pioneering a new art, it will at times necessarily produce power or commodities as a by-product. But they must be a by-product of the major purpose, not the major purpose itself.

Nor do I wish to be misinterpreted as believing that the United States is free-for-all and devil-take-the-hindmost. The very essence of equality of opportunity and of American individualism is that there shall be no domination by any group or combination in this republic, whether it be business or political. On the contrary, it demands economic justice as well as political and social justice. It is no system of laissez faire.

I feel deeply on this subject because during the war I had some practical experience with governmental operation and control. I have witnessed not only at home but abroad the many failures of government in business. I have seen its tyrannies, its injustices, its destructions of self-government, its undermining of the very instincts which carry our people forward to progress. I have witnessed the lack of advance, the lowered standards of living, the depressed spirits of people working under such a system. My objection is based not upon theory or upon a failure to recognize wrong or abuse, but I know the adoption of such methods would strike at the very roots of American life and would destroy the very basis of American progress.

Our people have the right to know whether we can continue to solve our great problems without abandonment of our American system. I know we can. . . .

And what have been the results of the American system? Our country has become the land of opportunity to those born without inheritance, not merely because of the wealth of its resources and industry but because of this freedom of initiative and enterprise. Russia has natural resources equal to ours. Her people are equally industrious, but she has not had the blessings of one hundred and fifty years of our form of government and our social system.

By adherence to the principles of decentralized self-government, ordered liberty, equal opportunity, and freedom to the individual, our American experiment in human welfare has yielded a degree of well-being unparalleled in all the world. It has come nearer to the abolition of poverty, to the abolition of fear of want, than humanity has ever reached before. Progress of the past seven years is the proof of it. This alone furnishes the answer to our opponents, who ask us to introduce destructive elements into the system by which this has been accomplished. . . .

I have endeavored to present to you that the greatness of America has grown out of a political and social system and a method of control of economic forces distinctly its own—our American system—which has carried this great experiment in human welfare farther than ever before in all history. We are nearer today to the ideal of the abolition of poverty and fear from the lives of men and women than ever before in any land. And I again repeat that the departure from our American system by injecting principles destructive to it which our opponents propose, will jeopardize the very liberty and freedom of our people, and will destroy equality of opportunity not alone to ourselves but to our children. . . .

[From *The New Day: Campaign Speeches of Herbert Hoover* (Stanford, Calif.: Stanford University Press, 1928), p. 149*ff*]

Questions for Reflection

To support his arguments for "rugged individualism," Hoover cites economic "progress of the past seven years." How would you assess the health of the American economy in the mid to late 1920s? Do you agree or disagree with Hoover on this point?

Is Hoover fair in his characterization of the Democratic program? How would you describe the philosophy of the Democrats in 1928? Do you agree with Hoover that the government should be "an umpire instead of a player in the economic game"?

ANSWERS TO MULTIPLE-CHOICE AND TRUE-FALSE QUESTIONS

Multiple-Choice Questions

1-D, 2-B, 3-D, 4-D, 5-B, 6-B, 7-D, 8-B

True-False Questions

1-F, 2-T, 3-F, 4-F, 5-T, 6-F, 7-F, 8-F

27

FRANKLIN D. ROOSEVELT
AND THE NEW DEAL

CHAPTER OBJECTIVES

After you complete the reading and study of this chapter you should be able to

1. Describe the character and appeal of FDR.
2. Describe the sources of New Deal legislation.
3. Explain the New Deal approaches to the problems of recovery in industry and agriculture.
4. Describe the criticisms made of the New Deal by the left and the right.
5. Describe New Deal efforts to deal with unemployment and welfare.
6. Assess the changes in the United States wrought by the New Deal.

CHAPTER OUTLINE

I. The election of 1932
   A. The candidates
   B. Roosevelt's background and character
   C. The campaign contrasts
   D. Results of the election

II. The early New Deal
   A. Mood of the inauguration
   B. Willingness to experiment
   C. Action for banks, the economy, and beer

   D. Overview of the Hundred Days
   E. Measures to improve financial institutions
      1. Extension of farm credit
      2. Help for home mortgages
      3. Action to protect banks and security purchases
      4. Abandonment of the gold standard
   F. Relief measures
      1. Civilian Conservation Corps (CCC)
      2. Federal Emergency Relief Administration (FERA)
      3. Civilian Works Administration (CWA)
      4. Works Progress Administration (WPA)

III. Recovery through regulation and planning
   A. Aid for agriculture
      1. Wide variety of options within the Agricultural Adjustment Administration (AAA)
      2. Creation of the Commodity Credit Corporation
      3. General effects on farm income and farmers
      4. Dust Bowl and migration
      5. Supreme Court negates the processing tax of AAA

   6. Soil Conservation Act: provisions
      and effects
   7. Second AAA
 B. Efforts for the recovery of industry
   1. The Public Works Administration
      (PWA)
   2. The National Recovery
      Administration (NRA)
      a. Two primary aims
      b. Nature of the NRA operation
      c. Objections to the NRA codes
      d. Enduring impact of the NRA
 C. Regional planning: Tennessee Valley
    Authority (TVA)
   1. Historical basis
   2. Nature of the legislation
   3. Impact of the TVA
   4. Creation of the Rural
      Electrification Association (REA)

IV. Critics left and right
 A. Increased support for FDR in 1934
 B. Conservatives launch the American
    Liberty League
 C. Thunder on the left
   1. Huey Long's threat
   2. Francis Townsend's program
   3. Father Coughlin's role
   4. Potential threat of the left
 D. Pressure on FDR to restore
    competition
 E. Roadblocks from the Supreme Court

V. The Second New Deal
 A. The Wagner Act for workers
 B. The Social Security Act
   1. Old Age and Survivors' Insurance
   2. Unemployment Insurance
   3. Public Assistance Programs
   4. Limitations
 C. The Wealth Tax Act
 D. Right-wing criticisms of the New Deal

VI. The election of 1936
 A. Contribution of Eleanor Roosevelt
 B. Republicans choose progressive Al
    Landon

 C. Republican strategy
 D. The new Roosevelt coalition
 E. Results of the election

VII. Second-term developments
 A. The court-packing plan
   1. FDR's view of the election
   2. Effects of Court rulings
   3. The court-packing plan
   4. Events blunt the plan
   5. Impact of the fight
 B. Stirrings among labor
   1. Impetus to unionization
   2. Rise of industrial unions
   3. Intense conflict with management
      a. Techniques used by
         management
      b. The sitdown strike
      c. CIO victories
      d. Growing power for organized
         labor
 C. Reaction to a new depression
   1. Course of the 1937 slump
   2. Administration's reaction
   3. The battle over policy
      a. Fear of the unbalanced budget
      b. A move from regulation to
         antitrust action
   4. Roosevelt's call for spending
   5. Reforms of 1937 and 1938
      a. Housing legislation
      b. Assistance for tenant farmers
      c. Fair Labor Standards Act
 D. Setbacks to the New Deal
   1. Emergence of an opposition
      a. Defection of the southerners
      b. Victories of the opposition in
         1938
   2. Roosevelt's 1938 purge
   3. Results of the 1938 elections
   4. Limited legislation in 1939

VIII. Impact of the New Deal
 A. Some enduring changes
 B. A course between extremes
 C. Creation of the "broker state"

KEY ITEMS OF CHRONOLOGY

TERMS TO MASTER

Listed below are some important terms or people with which you should be familiar after you complete the study of this chapter. Explain the significance of each name or term.

1. The Hundred Days
2. brain trust
3. Securities and Exchange Commission
4. Civilian Conservation Corps
5. Agricultural Adjustment Administration
6. "Dust Bowl"
7. "Okies"
8. *United States v. Butler*
9. Soil Conservation Act
10. Public Works Administration
11. Tennessee Valley Authority
12. Huey Long
13. *Schechter Poultry Corp. v. United States*
14. Wagner Act
15. Social Security Act
16. court-packing plan
17. CIO
18. John L. Lewis
19. Fair Labor Standards Act
20. broker state

VOCABULARY BUILDING

Listed below are some words used in this chapter. Look up each word in your dictionary.

1. ebullient
2. requisite
3. sallow
4. dole
5. purge
6. consummate
7. panacea
8. galvanized
9. surrogate
10. malevolent

EXERCISES FOR UNDERSTANDING

When you have completed reading the chapter, answer each of the following questions. If you have difficulty, go back and reread the section of the chapter related to the question.

Multiple-Choice Questions

Select the letter of the response that best completes the statement.

1. Before becoming president, Franklin Roosevelt had
   A. suffered from polio.
   B. never run for national political office.
   C. served as a U. S. senator.
   D. all of the above

2. In 1933 the New Deal immediately attacked problems in
   A. race relations.
   B. banking and finance.
   C. labor.
   D. diplomacy with Germany.

3. The Okies were
   A. refugees from the Dust Bowl.
   B. migrants from Oklahoma, Arkansas, Texas, and Missouri.
   C. overwhelmingly white people.
   D. all of the above

4. The National Industrial Recovery Act provided for
   A. $3.3 billion in spending through the PWA.
   B. codes of fair practice for industries.
   C. the right of workers to form unions.
   D. all of the above

5. The New Deal's "cornerstone" and "supreme achievement," according to FDR, was
   A. Social Security.
   B. the Wagner Labor Relations Act.
   C. the Tennessee Valley Authority.
   D. the PWA and WPA.

6. Eleanor Roosevelt helped her husband most by
   A. remaining discreetly noncontroversial.
   B. maintaining ties to blacks and labor.
   C. pulling him toward more conservative policies.
   D. going on diplomatic missions to Asia and Africa.

7. The Supreme Court–packing plan was defeated in part because of
   A. Democratic losses in 1936.

B. its violation of the Constitution.
C. a change in the Court's direction in rulings on key measures.
D. all of the above

8. The momentum of FDR and the New Deal was hurt by
    A. the election of 1936.
    B. the failure of CIO efforts in the auto and steel industries.
    C. a second attack of polio.
    D. the recession of 1937.

True-False Questions

Indicate whether each statement is true or false.

1. In his 1932 campaign, FDR spelled out in detail his plans for fighting the depression.
2. The U.S. abandoned the gold standard for its money in 1933.
3. The AAA of 1933 tried to help farmers by getting them to reduce production.
4. FDR preferred work-relief to the dole.
5. The Social Security tax did "soak the rich."
6. The GOP candidate in 1936 was a longtime opponent of the entire New Deal.
7. Perhaps the most enduring voting change brought by FDR was the shift of the farm vote to the Democratic party.
8. An innovation in labor unions in the 1930s involved organizing workers in entire industries into the same union.

DOCUMENT

Excerpts from the Federal Writers Project Interviews with Depression Victims

Through the efforts of New Deal agencies Americans learned much about themselves in the 1930s. The Federal Writers Project, for instance, published poignant accounts of the lives of people in some southern states.

A Match of New Deal Agencies

The New Deal period witnessed the creation of a plethora of new government agencies which became known as the alphabet agencies because they were referred to by their initials. To help you focus on major agencies and to test your grasp of the material, on the following pages, match the description or statement on the right with the agencies or act on the left. Some of the agencies or acts may match with more than one description. Answers are at the end of this chapter.

Essay Questions

1. What special qualities did Franklin Roosevelt bring to the presidency?
2. How did the "first" and "second" New Deals differ? How were they similar?
3. Compare and contrast the New Deal's policies toward labor and agriculture.
4. What were the three or four most important programs of the New Deal? Explain your choices.
5. What factors in 1937 and 1938 contributed to a decline of the New Deal?
6. Evaluate the long-term significance of the New Deal.

The excerpts below come from those accounts. You may wish to compare them with the accounts in Chapter 20 of industrial workers in Illinois in the 1880s.

Agency or Act	Description
1. FDIC	a. created a regional rehabilitation of a river basin
2. FERA	b. investigated the concentration of economic power in the United States
3. Economy Act	c. set minimum wages and maximum hours for certain industries in interstate commerce
4. First AAA	d. provided a variety of methods for increasing farm income
5. Civilian Conservation Corps	e. provided insurance for bank deposits
6. PWA	f. provided $3.3 billion for jobs on major building projects
7. TVA	g. established a stopgap plan for aiding the unemployed from 1933 to 1935
8. NRA	h. provided loans to rural cooperatives to run electrical lines to remote farms
9. REA	i. established a plan to cut wages of veterans and federal employees
10. Wagner Act	j. provided jobs for young men in the nation's parks
11. Social Security Act	k. regulated the sale of stocks and bonds
12. Wealth Tax Act	l. allowed industries to collaborate together to limit production of goods and raise wages
13. SEC	m. provided farmers payments to conserve soil by not planting crops
14. TNEC	n. created a committee to oversee elections for unions

Agency or Act	Description
15. Farm Security Administration	o. established the welfare system for mothers and dependent children
16. Soil Conservation Act	p. greatly increased income taxes
17. Fair Labor Standards Act	q. provided a tax on incomes to ensure retirement benefits
18. WPA	r. placed a tax on farm products when first processed for market
	s. provided loans to help farm tenants buy their land
	t. established a long-term federal program to provide jobs, including in symphony orchestras, and in artistic and theater projects
	u. provided aid to the states for work projects as well as a dole
	v. built dams to produce and sell electricity
	w. a counterpart to NRA, this agency provided jobs on major construction projects

From the Account of a White Brick-Plant Worker and His Washer-Woman Wife

"Hub's hired solid time and has been for two years. He works every day from six in the morning till six at night in Mr. Hunter's brick plant across the tracks. Some days more'n that—twenty-four hours on a stretch. That's over-time, but it don't mean no extra pay. It's forty dollars a month straight, no matter what."

Rena Murray—small, stooped, hollow-chested—put her whole ninety pounds behind the heavy flatiron. Collar and cuffs came from under the heat, stiff and slick. She lifted the shirt from the board for final inspection.

"Hub fires the boiler most of the time. Then when they're drying bricks, he has to run the fan for twenty-four hours. They couldn't make out in that kiln unless Hub was there.

"He ought to git more for the work he puts out. Forty dollars a month just ain't enough for us to live on. Me and Hub and the three children. We have to pay four dollars out every month for this shack. Mr. Hunter makes the hands live close by the plant. And he gits ahold of that four dollars for rent before we ever see a cent of Hub's wages. This shack ain't worth four dollars a month, neither. Mr. Hunter won't do nothing toward fixing it up. If a window pane's broke, we do the putting in. Leak done ruint the paper and it's up to us to see to new paper."

Rena stooped to the tub of sprinkled clothes. She shook out a rolled-up bundle and slipped another shirt over the narrow end of the home-made ironing board. She settled the board again between the center table and the lard bucket set in a backless kitchen chair.

"I take in washing or do what I can to help out."

"We ain't been to church for years. I was taught working on Sunday was wrong. Folks that holds out against working on Sunday don't have to hire others to work for 'em if they don't show up. Hub had to pay a dollar and a quarter yesterday to git a man to turn the fan so's he could see after his sister. She's about to die. Dirty shame for a man to have to pay to go see his own die. I sure wish he could find hisself a better job."

"What he aims to do is to turn over every stone he can to git back on the WPA. We got along a lot better on the WPA. We had our check regular and had good warm clothes for the girls. And they give Hub clothes, too, because his work kept him in the open. I didn't git none but I could manage all right when the others was gitting all they did. Whenever one of us would git down, the WPA would send a doctor and medicine. They give us food, too. Things that are supposed to be healthy for eating such as prunes and raisins. We can't buy 'em now."

"Burial insurance is a good thing. I wish I had a policy on me and every one of the children. That's just wishing. It pinches us plumb to death to keep Hub's going. We was always behind in dues till he got put on solid time. I couldn't git no insurance noways on account of my bad health. I've had the pneumonia since we've been here. Down three months. There wasn't a Hunter had feeling enough to set foot in this shack. Mrs. Hunter has spoke to me times since, but Mr. Hunter don't trouble about speaking to them that slaves for him. My mammy taught me a dog was good enough to be nice to."

From the Account of a Young Shoe-Factory Worker

"My work is hard all right. It's hard on me because I ain't but only seventeen and ain't got my full growth yet. It's work down in the steam room which they call it that because it's always full of steam which sometimes when you go in it you can't hardly see. You steam leather down there and that steam soaks you clean to the skin. It makes me keep a cold most of the time because when I go out doors I'm sopping wet. Another thing that's hard about it is having so much standing up to do. My hours is from seven o'clock in the morning till four in the evening. And it's stand on my feet the whole time. When noon time comes and I'm off an hour, why I just find me somewheres to set and I sure set there. You couldn't pay me to stand up during lunch time.

"I'm on piecework now and I can't seem to get my production up to where I make just a whole lot. You get paid by the production hour and it takes fifty pair of shoes to make that hour. You get forty-two cents for the hour. Highest I ever made in one week was eleven dollars and the lowest was seven dollars and forty-two cents. I usually hit in between and make eight or nine dollars.

"Now and then somebody will say, 'We ought to have us a union here of some sort.' That kind of talk just makes me mad all over. Mr. Pugh is a Christian man. He brought his factory here to give us some work which we didn't have any before. We do pretty well, I think, to just stay away from that kind of talk. All but the sore-heads and trouble-makers is satisfied and glad to have work.

"I don't blame Mr. Pugh a bit the way he feels about the unions. The plant manager knows Mr. Pugh mighty well and he told my foreman what Mr. Pugh said. Mr. Pugh said, 'If the union ever comes in here and I have to operate my plant under a union, why I'll just close the plant down and move it away from Hancock so quick it'll make your head swim.' That's his word on it and I don't blame him none. I'd hate to see a union try here. No plant and no jobs for anybody. They just operate these unions out of Wall Street, anyhow, trying to ruin people like Mr. Pugh. . . .

"My money has to go a long way. I've got to pay eight dollars a month rent and I have to buy coal and stove wood. I got to buy clothes for the family and something to eat for them. Then twice a month there's that five dollar ambulance bill which it's to take my brother that's got the T.B. to the City Hospital in Memphis where they take and drain his lungs. Sure charge you for an ambulance, don't they? Now, some people say if you just take one trip in an ambulance, the undertaker won't ask a cent for it. Figures he'll get your custom if you pass on. But they sure charge me for my brother.

"Well, I'm always glad when it's quitting time. I like to work there, but you can't help getting tired. I go on home. I walk four blocks and I'm there. Usually I have to wait a while for supper so I just set at the window. I like to watch and see if maybe something will come along the street and I can watch it. Sometimes there's a new funny paper there and I will look it over—specially if it's Tarzan. That's the best thing in a funny paper, the Tarzan part. Nobody ever gets it over old Tarzan, do they? Most times, though, I like to just set there and watch."

"I work steady but I'm most always financially in need of money. It takes a lot to keep a family going. My little sister needs glasses but they cost too much. All of my family has weak eyes but we can't afford to wear glasses.

"So I haven't the money for running around. I wouldn't if I had the money, either. The Bible is against running around and playing cards and seeing the moving pictures. People should study their Bible more and we'd have more Christian men like Mr. Pugh and more jobs. So me and a young lady I know of go to church and Sunday School instead of running around. My family belongs to the Baptist Church, but this certain young lady is a Nazarene and that's where we go.

"You know, when you're blue and down at the mouth and don't

see any use anyhow, a good sermon just lifts you up. You haven't got a thing to lose by living a Christian life. Take Mr. Pugh. He lives it and look where he is now. And if you don't make out that way, if you're poor all your life, then you get a high place in the Kingdom. Just do the best you know how and the Lord will take care of you either here or hereafter. It sure is a comfort."

From the Account of a Young Man in Charge of a WPA Supply Room

"The way I look at it is this. This is a rich country. I figger it ain't going to hurt the government to feed and clothe them that needs it. Half of 'em can't get work, or just ain't fixed to handle work if they get it. I imagine this country's worth near on to ten billion dollars. We've got the money. Plenty of it. No sense in the big fellows kicking about a little handout to the poor. Matter's not if some ain't deserving.

"I'll admit there's some don't deserve a nickel of the government's money. Lot of them that comes here, why I'd sooner give them a kick in the pants than shove 'em out supplies. But you got to take the good with the bad. Or bad with the good, whichever way you've a mind to put it. Most that comes here are poor and can't help it. Needs help. Needs it just same I need this job. Always going to be more poor folks than them that ain't poor. Now take me. I've always been poor and I guess I always will be. I ain't saying that's the government's fault. It's just a downright truth, that's all.

"There's a lot of things I'd like different in the world. But I can't say I got so much to complain of. If I'd had more education like as not I'd be getting more pay. Maybe, I wouldn't. Not getting no schooling is my own fault. Poor or rich, humans is faulty one way or the next. Time I got to the seventh grade I got the making of money in my head. Wages looked to be about the best thing in the world. Well, I had a run of good jobs. Made fair money for a year or two driving trucks. Took a turn at auto fixing, too, around a filling station. Just first one thing and another. Jobs was easy to get then. That's before women got set on going to work. That's what caused all this depression business. I'm not saying that the women don't need jobs now. They does. But they got themselves to thank for the fix the world's in. They started out taking jobs from men when there wasn't no sense in them working. Them men lost out on good jobs and dropped right down and took ours. Just wasn't no jobs left for poor folks.

"Folks that ain't never been poor just don't know nothin' a-tall about doing on nothing. I get so all-fired full of laugh when some of these women from the higher ups comes down to the Welfare Department. Nice ladies, but it ain't a salt spoon of sense about poor folks in their heads. Pretty little thing come last week to tell the women come here about cooking. Before she started spieling, she seen them cans of salmon I took from the big case and put on that shelf back there. That give her a start. She aimed to tell them how to make up a pot dish from salmon. We ain't really got no salmon here. Just a cheap grade of canned mackerel. She sailed in. 'Brush the baking dish with melted butter,' says she. If she hadn't been so pretty and so young, I'd liked to asked right off—'Where they going to get the butter? Ain't two in the room's got butter for their bread. You'll have to shift to a skillet for the cooking. That's about the best they got for greasing up.' Of course I didn't say no such to her. She was just plumb wore out time she got that salmon out of her head and into the cook stove. When she come to tail part of the talk giving them leave to ask her questions, she looked to me about ready to fall off the box I'd drug out for her to speak from. It's a blessing the Lord made it easy for some. A blessing. And I'm glad He done it."

"Asides from groceries and rent and clothes there's ten dollars a week wages. I figger our spending, all told, about twenty dollars a month. Things we got to have that ain't give us is bought on the installment plan. Cost more that way. But what you going to do when things got to be got and there's no spot cash to hand! We's pulling long through debt right well. Just fifteen dollars owing on the furniture and about twenty-five on the washing machine. Lord, that washing machine's worth ever cent we paid for it. I told Ella if I ever seen another thing that'd be as big help to her I'd buy it if I had to bust a bank. It don't take her half the time used to to get all them youngun's clothes did and the house things and such. Ella keep everthing from the kids to the kivers clean as a pin. House the same. We keep our kids close to home. Don't let them run round with just any trash. I got the last one of ours insured for burial— except sister. I'll get her fixed time she's year old. I pay twenty cents a week on me and Ella. Ten cents for the two oldest boys, five cents for the others.

"Thing that worries me most about a large family is the feeding of them right. I know ours don't have what they's supposed to. Not if half's right I hear them ladies who come here to talk says. We can't manage the milk we should for them. If we get Grade A they ain't enough for more than a cup around. I guess that cheap canned milk's good enough for cooking. We uses what they give us. Them things concocted for the place of butter ain't as cheap as you'd think. I ain't strong like I used to be. And with all this talk I hear floating round I wonder if its the things I ain't had to eat that'd done it."

From the Account of a CCC Boy

"I ain't never been much to school. Jist went to the second grade, that's all, excepting what I learned here in the CCC. I could have gone, I guess, but for some reason didn't keer nothing about it. Jist didn't want to go. I would have went if I wanted to. They didn't make me not go. We jist didn't none of us go. I got one brother that went to the second grade, too, and my sister she went to the first. Then she quit. We jist wasn't a family that like school.

"I quit that old second grade when I was fourteen. I left home and went to work. Been on my own ever since. I went down here to Woolard and went to work on a farm. The man he was sick and not able to work and had to have somebody to help him. That's why I got to work so long, and even got the job at all. Got twenty dollars a month."

I asked, "Would you go on to school and finish now if you had the chance?"

"Don't know whether I could or not. I would really like to learn." He flushed and scowled. "The boys they make fun of us when we can't read the funnies nor nothing. I look at pictures in books, and things like that in the recreation hall, so they won't laugh at me. I wish I had gone on to school now and would go as far as I could if I git the chance. Guess I couldn't git much learning now though, could I? I'm too old most to learn now."

I asked if he wanted to stay with the CCC.

"Yes'm, as long as I kin, because I git plenty to eat here. I didn't always at home, not the same kind of stuff, anyhow. Guess we had plenty, such as it was, at home, but it jist wasn't good like this, nor enough of it for the kind it was. I git to go more, git to see more. I'm learning too. I watch the others, and then, I have more clothes and can keep cleaner too."

"Do I go to church?

"Well, no'm. Not now. But while in the C's I do. The chaplain preaches to us two times a month, and I like to hear him. He makes tears come in my eyes, too. I quit drinking all on account of him. I'm a good boy now. I don't go to church at town much because I'm afraid they'll laugh at me. My mother she's a Baptist, but I jist go to any of them. I always give some money when I have it to give.

"Down home it's different. I've rambled all over that place and they ain't got no churches down there. I been there two years and ain't ever seen no church yet. Some of my little brothers ain't never seen no church yet."

[From *These Are Our Lives* (1939), as told to and written by members of the Federal Writers' Project of the W.P.A. (New York: W. W. Norton & Co., 1975), pp. 224–228, 231–235, 366–368, 412– 414]

Questions for Reflection

Compare the wages and expenses of these workers. Which one seems to be better situated financially? What role does religion play in the lives of these people? How do they feel about their "bosses" and others in positions superior to them? Whom do they blame for their financial difficulties? What was the attitude of the shoe-factory worker toward labor unions? One of the benefits of the New Deal was improved public education on nutrition. What evidence do you find in these accounts of nutritional awareness? What evidence is there that the advice of government social workers to the poor was impractical?

How do these accounts of workers' lives compare with those of the 1880s Illinois workers in Chapter 20?

ANSWERS TO MULTIPLE-CHOICE, TRUE-FALSE, AND MATCHING QUESTIONS

Multiple-Choice Questions

1-A, 2-B, 3-D, 4-D, 5-A, 6-B, 7-C, 8-D

True-False Questions

1-F, 2-T, 3-T, 4-T, 5-F, 6-F, 7-F, 8-T

Matching Questions

1-e, 2-q,u, 3-i, 4-d,r, 5-j, 6-f,w, 7-a,v, 8-l,
9-h, 10-n, 11-o,q, 12-p, 13-k, 14-b, 15-s,
16-m, 17-c, 18-t

28

FROM ISOLATION TO GLOBAL WAR

CHAPTER OBJECTIVES

After you complete the reading and study of this chapter you should be able to

1. Explain and account for the foreign policy pursued by the United States in the interwar period.
2. Describe the aggressions of Japan, Italy, and Germany in the decade of the 1930s.
3. Account for American efforts at neutrality in the face of aggression and assess the effectiveness of neutrality in preventing war.
4. Describe the election of 1940.
5. Explain American support of Britain and Russia prior to the United States's entry into the war.
6. Explain and account for the effectiveness of the attack on Pearl Harbor.

CHAPTER OUTLINE

I. Postwar isolationism
  A. Evidences of isolationist sentiment
  B. Counteractions of world involvement
  C. Relations with the League
  D. The war-debt tangle
    1. Problems with repayment of debts
    2. Linkage of debts to reparations
    3. Depression and debt cancellation

E. Efforts toward disarmament
    1. A substitute for League membership
    2. Strained Japanese-American relations
    3. The Washington Armaments Conference
      a. Hughes's initiative
      b. Agreements made at the conference
      c. Effects of the treaties
    4. The movement to outlaw war
      a. Development of the Kellogg-Briand Pact
      b. Effect of the pact
  F. The "Good-Neighbor" Policy
    1. Early efforts to improve relations with Latin America
    2. Hoover and the Clark Memorandum
    3. Further improvements under FDR

II. War clouds
  A. Japanese incursion in China
    1. Chinese weaknesses
    2. Japanese occupation of Manchuria
    3. Reactions to occupation
      a. League condemnation
      b. Japan's withdrawal from the League
  B. Mussolini's rise to power
  C. Hitler's rise to power
  D. American recognition of the Soviet Union

E. Aggression in Asia and Europe
 1. Italian invasion of Ethiopia, 1935
 2. Hitler's occupation of the
    Rhineland, 1936
 3. Spanish Civil War, 1936
 4. Japanese invasion of China, 1937
 5. Hitler's *Anschluss* with Austria,
    1938
 6. The Munich Agreement, 1938
 7. War begun over Poland, 1939

III. American efforts for neutrality
 A. The Nye Committee investigations
 B. Congressional effort to avoid another
    world war
 C. The first Neutrality Act, 1935
  1. Sale of arms to belligerents
     forbidden
  2. Travel discouraged on belligerent
     ships
 D. Reaction to the invasion of Ethiopia
 E. The second Neutrality Act: loans to
    belligerents forbidden
 F. Extension of the Neutrality Act to
    cover civil wars
 G. Further neutrality provisions
 H. Reactions to Japanese action in China
  1. Lack of use of neutrality laws
  2. Quarantine speech
 I. Reactions to war in Europe
  1. Change to cash-and-carry arms
     sales
  2. Extension of war zone

IV. The storm in Europe
 A. Hitler's *Blitzkrieg*
 B. American aid to embattled Britain

 1. Growth of U.S. defense effort
 2. Sales of arms to Britain
C. Other defense measures
D. The destroyer-bases deal
E. Peacetime conscription
F. Polarization of public opinion
 1. Committee to Defend America
 2. America First Committee

V. The election of 1940
 A. The choice of Willkie
 B. The choice of FDR
 C. Nature of the campaign
 D. Results of the election

VI. The arsenal of democracy
 A. The Lend-Lease program
 B. Further Axis gains
 C. Reaction to the invasion of the Soviet
    Union
 D. The Atlantic Charter
 E. Conflict with the Germans in the
    Atlantic

VII. The storm in the Pacific
 A. Japanese aggression in Southeast Asia
 B. Tripartite Pact
 C. Negotiations between Japan and the
    United States
 D. Warlords gain control in Japan
 E. Attack on Pearl Harbor
  1. Extent of U.S. foreknowledge
  2. Errors in warning
  3. Damage from the attack
  4. Other Japanese aggression in the
     Pacific
 F. Declaration of war

KEY ITEMS OF CHRONOLOGY

Washington Disarmament Conference	1921–1922
Mussolini took power in Italy	1925
Kellogg-Briand Pact	1928
Japanese invasion of Manchuria	1931
Hitler took power in Germany	1933
London Economic Conference	1933
Nye Committee	1934–1937
Italy's invasion of Ethiopia	1935
Japan's invasion of China	1937
Quarantine Speech	1937
World War II began	September 1, 1939
First peacetime draft	1940

Fall of France	June 1940
Lend-Lease program began	1941
Germany's invasion of Russia	June 1941
Japanese extend protectorate over Indochina	July 1941
Attack on Pearl Harbor	December 7, 1941

TERMS TO MASTER

Listed below are some important terms or people with which you should be familiar after you complete the study of this chapter. Explain the significance of each name or term.

1. World Court
2. Washington Armaments Conference
3. reparations
4. Five-Power Treaty
5. Kellogg-Briand Pact
6. Good-Neighbor Policy
7. London Naval Conference
8. Cordell Hull
9. Reciprocal Trade Agreements
10. Nye Committee
11. Neutrality Acts
12. cash and carry
13. *Blitzkrieg*
14. America First Committee
15. Wendell Willkie
16. Lend-Lease program
17. Four Freedoms
18. Atlantic Charter

VOCABULARY BUILDING

Listed below are some words used in this chapter. Look up each word in your dictionary.

1. reparations
2. encroachments
3. partition
4. allay
5. abrogate
6. incursion
7. fascist
8. ludicrous
9. brazenly
10. embargo

EXERCISES FOR UNDERSTANDING

When you have completed reading the chapter, answer each of the following questions. If you have difficulty, go back and reread the section of the chapter related to the question.

Multiple-Choice Questions

Select the letter of the response that best completes the statement.

1. America's involvement with the rest of the world was assured in the 1920s by
   A. the wordwide connections of American business.
   B. American investments and loans abroad.
   C. United States possessions in the Pacific.
   D. all of the above

2. The naval armaments race after World War I came in response to
   A. the rise of Hitler.
   B. British expansion in East Asia and the Pacific.
   C. the Harding administration's commitment to a big navy.
   D. the growing power of Japan.

3. In the early 1930s Roosevelt's foreign policy included
   A. advocacy of U.S. membership in the League of Nations.
   B. proposals to deal with the depression on an international scale.
   C. reciprocal trade agreements.
   D. all of the above

4. The Nye Committee investigations seemed to prove that
   A. the United States entered World War I to permit the munitions manufacturers to make greater profits.

B. the United States should back down from its dispute with Japan over China.

C. the only way to end the war was with a treaty.

D. the United States was not responsible for the success of the attack by Japan.

5. The Neutrality Act of 1939
   A. prohibited all trade with belligerents.
   B. allowed trade with only one side in a war.
   C. kept U.S. ships from war zones but approved cash-and-carry trade even for arms.
   D. permitted nonmilitary trade in American ships only.

6. In the summer of 1940
   A. the United States and Britain swapped destroyers for naval and air bases.
   B. Congress appropriated $4 billion for a two-ocean navy.
   C. the first peacetime draft became law.
   D. all of the above occurred

7. The Atlantic Charter of 1941
   A. declared British-American war aims.
   B. ordered German U-boats out of the Atlantic.
   C. ended U.S. neutrality on the seas and led to conflict with Germany.
   D. reaffirmed the Kellogg-Briand Pact.

8. The Japanese attack on Pearl Harbor
   A. was a complete success.
   B. sunk or severely damaged all U.S. aircraft carriers in the Pacific.
   C. killed 25,000 Americans.
   D. missed vital shore installations and oil tanks.

True-False Questions

Indicate whether each statement is true or false.

1. America's allies in World War I had paid all their war debts by 1924.
2. The Kellogg-Briand Pact provided for multinational attacks on any nation which started a war.
3. The Clark Memorandum attacked the Japanese invasion of Korea.
4. The United States gave diplomatic recognition to the Soviet Union in 1933.
5. The United States tried to avoid World War II by outlawing the supposed causes of World War I.
6. The America First Committee advocated aid to Great Britain.
7. In 1941 the Lend-Lease program concentrated on stopping Italian conquests in Eastern Europe.
8. The United States declaration of war in 1941 passed the Congress unanimously.

Essay Questions

1. Was the United States more isolationist in its foreign policy during 1920–1929 or 1930–1939? Explain.
2. Describe American efforts to achieve peace and disarmament during the 1920s.
3. Describe American efforts to improve relations with Latin America from 1921 through 1940.
4. How did the United States and the Allied nations react to Axis aggressions in the 1930s? Why?
5. Why did the United States seek to remain neutral in the 1930s?
6. Explain the importance of foreign policy issues in the election of 1940.
7. Account for the attack on Pearl Harbor in 1941 and assess its consequences.

DOCUMENTS

Document 1. Roosevelt's Quarantine Speech, 1937

In the wake of the rearmament of Germany, the Italian invasion of Ethiopia, the Spanish Civil War, and finally the Japanese invasion of China, Roosevelt visited Chicago, the heart of isolationist sentiment in America, on October 5, 1937, to make what has generally been dubbed his Quarantine Speech. Look carefully in the following excerpts for the promises or pledges that the president sought to exact on the issues of peace and war.

> I am glad to come once again to Chicago and especially to have the opportunity of taking part in the dedication of this important project of civic betterment. . . .
>
> Without a declaration of war and without warning or justification of any kind, civilians, including women and children, are being ruthlessly murdered with bombs from the air. In times of so-called peace ships are being attacked and sunk by submarines without cause or notice. Nations are fomenting and taking sides in civil warfare in nations that have never done them any harm. Nations claiming freedom for themselves deny it to others. . . .
>
> The peace-loving nations must make a concerted effort in opposition to those violations of treaties and those ignorings of humane instincts which today are creating a state of international anarchy and instability from which there is no escape through mere isolation or neutrality. . . .
>
> There is a solidarity and interdependence about the modern world, both technically and morally, which makes it impossible for any nation completely to isolate itself from economic and political upheavals in the rest of the world, specially when such upheavals appear to be spreading and not declining.
>
> It seems to be unfortunately true that the epidemic of world lawlessness is spreading.
>
> When an epidemic of physical disease starts to spread, the community approves and joins in a quarantine of the patients in order to protect the health of the community against the spread of the disease.
>
> War is a contagion, whether it be declared or undeclared. It can engulf states and peoples remote from the original scene of hostilities. . . . We are adopting such measures as will minimize our risk of involvement, but we cannot have complete protection in a world of disorder in which confidence and security have broken down.
>
> If civilization is to survive the principles of the Prince of Peace must be restored. Shattered trust between nations must be revived.
>
> Most important of all, the will for peace on the part of peace-loving nations must express itself to the end that nations that may be tempted to violate their agreements and the rights of others will desist from such a cause. There must be positive endeavors to preserve peace.
>
> America hates war. America hopes for peace. Therefore, America actively engages in the search for peace.
>
> [U.S. Department of State, *Peace and War: United States Foreign Policy, 1931–1941* (Washington, D.C.: U.S. Government Printing Office, 1943), pp. 384–387]

Document 2. Roosevelt's "Four Freedoms" Speech, 1941

The "Four Freedoms," formulated in Roosevelt's annual message to Congress on January 6, 1941, have come to be accepted as the most succinct statement of the things for which the American people were prepared to fight.

To the Congress of the United States:

I address you, the Members of the Seventy-Seventh Congress, at a moment unprecedented in the history of the Union. I use the word "unprecedented," because at no previous time has American security been as seriously threatened from without as it is today.
. . .

It is true that prior to 1914 the United States often had been disturbed by events in other Continents. We had even engaged in two wars with European nations and in a number of undeclared wars in the West Indies, in the Mediterranean and in the Pacific for the maintenance of American rights and for the principles of peaceful commerce. In no case, however, had a serious threat been raised against our national safety or our independence.

What I seek to convey is the historic truth that the United States as a nation has at all times maintained opposition to any attempt to lock us in behind an ancient Chinese wall while the procession of civilization went past. Today, thinking of our children and their children, we oppose enforced isolation for ourselves or for any part of the Americas.

Even when the World War broke out in 1914, it seemed to contain only small threat of danger to our own American future. But, as time went on, the American people began to visualize what the downfall of democratic nations might mean to our own democracy.

We need not over-emphasize imperfections in the Peace of Versailles. We need not harp on failure of the democracies to deal with problems of world deconstruction. We should remember that the Peace of 1919 was far less unjust than the kind of "pacification" which began even before Munich, and which is being carried on under the new order of tyranny that seeks to spread over every continent today. The American people have unalterably set their faces against that tyranny.

Every realist knows that the democratic way of life is at this moment being directly assailed in every part of the world—assailed either by arms, or by secret spreading of poisonous propaganda by those who seek to destroy unity and promote discord in nations still at peace. During sixteen months this assault has blotted out the whole pattern of democratic life in an appalling number of independent nations, great and small. The assailants are still on the march, threatening other nations, great and small.

Therefore, as your President, performing my constitutional duty to "give to the Congress information of the state of the Union," I find it necessary to report that the future and the safety of our country and of our democracy are overwhelmingly involved in events far beyond our borders.

Armed defense of democratic existence is now being gallantly waged in four continents. If that defense fails, all the population and all the resources of Europe, Asia, Africa and Australasia will be dominated by the conquerors. The total of those populations and their resources greatly exceeds the sum total of the population and resources of the whole of the Western Hemisphere—many times over.

In times like these it is immature—and incidentally untrue—for anybody to brag that an unprepared America, single-handed, and with one hand tied behind its back, can hold off the whole world.

No realistic American can expect from a dictator's peace international generosity, or return of true independence, or world disarmament, or freedom of expression, or freedom of religion—or even good business. Such a peace would bring no security for us or for our neighbors. "Those, who would give up essential liberty to purchase a little temporary safety, deserve neither liberty nor safety." As a nation we may take pride in the fact that we are soft-hearted; but we cannot afford to be soft-hearted. We must always be wary of those who with sounding brass and a tinkling cymbal preach the "ism" of appeasement. We must especially beware of that small group of selfish men who would clip the wings of the American eagle in order to feather their own nests.

I have recently pointed out how quickly the tempo of modern warfare could bring into our very midst the physical attack which we must expect if the dictator nations win this war.

There is much loose talk of our immunity from immediate and direct invasion from across the seas. Obviously, as long as the British Navy retains its power, no such danger exists. Even if there were no British Navy, it is not probable that any enemy would be stupid enough to attack us by landing troops in the United States from across thousands of miles of ocean, until it had acquired strategic bases from which to operate. But we learn much from the lessons of the past years in Europe—particularly the lesson of Norway, whose essential seaports were captured by treachery and surprise built up over a series of years. The first phase of the invasion of this Hemisphere would not be the landing of regular troops. The necessary strategic points would be occupied by secret agents and their dupes—and great numbers of them are already here, and in Latin America.

As long as the aggressor nations maintain the offensive, they—not we—will choose the time and the place and the method of their attack. That is why the future of all American Republics is today in serious danger. That is why this Annual Message to the Congress is unique in our history. That is why every member of the Executive branch of the government and every member of the Congress face great responsibility—and great accountability.

The need of the moment is that our actions and our policy should be devoted primarily—almost exclusively—to meeting this foreign peril. For all our domestic problems are now a part of the great emergency. Just as our national policy in internal affairs has been based upon a decent respect for the rights and dignity of all our fellowmen within our gates, so our national policy in foreign affairs has been based on a decent respect for the rights and dignity of all nations, large and small. And the justice of morality must and will win in the end.

Our national policy is this.

First, by an impressive expression of the public will and without regard to partisanship, we are committed to all-inclusive national defense.

Second, by an impressive expression of the public will and without regard to partisanship, we are committed to full support of all those resolute peoples, everywhere, who are resisting aggression and are thereby keeping war away from our Hemisphere. By this support, we express our determination that the democratic cause shall prevail; and we strengthen the defense and security of our own nation.

Third, by an impressive expression of the public will and without regard to partisanship, we are committed to the proposition that principles of morality and considerations for our own security will never permit us to acquiesce in a peace dictated by aggressors and sponsored by appeasers. We know that enduring peace cannot be bought at the cost of other people's freedom.

In the recent national election there was no substantial difference between the two great parties in respect to that national policy. No issue was fought out on this line before the American electorate. Today, it is abundantly evident that American citizens everywhere are demanding and supporting speedy and complete action in recognition of obvious danger. Therefore, the immediate need is a swift and driving increase in our armament production. . . .

Our most useful and immediate role is to act as an arsenal for them as well as for ourselves. They do not need man power. They do need billions of dollars worth of the weapons of defense. . . .

Let us say to the democracies: "We Americans are vitally concerned in your defense of freedom. We are putting forth our energies, our resources and our organizing powers to give you the strength to regain and maintain a free world. We shall send you, in ever-increasing numbers, ships, planes, tanks, guns. This is our purpose and our pledge." In fulfillment of this purpose we will not be intimidated by the threats of dictators that they will regard as a breach of international law and as an act of war our aid to the democracies which dare to resist their aggression. Such aid is not an act of war, even if a dictator should unilaterally proclaim it so to be. When the dictators are ready to make war upon us, they will not wait for an act of war on our part. They did not wait for Norway or Belgium or the Netherlands to commit an act of war. Their only interest is in a new one-way international law, which lacks mutuality in its observance, and, therefore, becomes an instrument of oppression.

The happiness of future generations of Americans may well depend upon how effective and how immediate we can make our aid felt. No one can tell the exact character of the emergency situations that we may be called upon to meet. The Nation's hands must not be tied when the Nation's life is in danger. We must all prepare to make the sacrifices that the emergency—as serious as war itself—demands. Whatever stands in the way of speed and efficiency in defense preparations must give way to the national need.

A free nation has the right to expect full cooperation from all groups. A free nation has the right to look to the leaders of business, of labor, and of agriculture to take the lead in stimulating effort, not among other groups but within their own groups. The best way of dealing with the few slackers or trouble makers in our midst is, first, to shame them by patriotic example, and, if that fails, to use the sovereignty of government to save government.

As men do not live by bread alone, they do not fight by armaments alone. Those who man our defenses, and those behind them who build our defenses, must have the stamina and courage which come from an unshakable belief in the manner of life which they are defending. The mighty action which we are calling for cannot be based on a disregard of all things worth fighting for.

The Nation takes great satisfaction and much strength from the things which have been done to make its people conscious of their individual stake in the preservation of democratic life in America. Those things have toughened the fibre of our people, have renewed their faith and strengthened their devotion to the institutions we make ready to protect. Certainly this is no time to stop thinking about the social and economic problems which are the root cause of the social revolution which is today a supreme factor in the world.

There is nothing mysterious about the foundations of a healthy and strong democracy. The basic things expected by our people of their political and economic systems are simple. They are: equality of opportunity for youth and for others; jobs for those who can work; security for those who need it; the ending of special privilege for the few; the preservation of civil liberties for all; the enjoyment of the fruits of scientific progress in a wider and constantly rising standard of living.

These are the simple and basic things that must never be lost sight of in the turmoil and unbelievable complexity of our modern world. The inner and abiding strength of our economic and political systems is dependent upon the degree to which they fulfill these expectations.

Many subjects connected with our social economy call for immediate improvement. As examples: We should bring more citizens under the coverage of old age pensions and unemployment insurance. We should widen the opportunities for adequate medical care. We should plan a better system by which persons deserving or needing gainful employment may obtain it.

I have called for personal sacrifice. I am assured of the willingness of almost all Americans to respond to that call. . . .

In the future days, which we seek to make secure, we look forward to a world founded upon four essential human freedoms.

The first is freedom of speech and expression—everywhere in the world.

The second is freedom of every person to worship God in his own way—everywhere in the world.

The third is freedom from want—which, translated into world terms, means economic understandings which will secure to every nation a healthy peace time life for its inhabitants—everywhere in the world.

The fourth is freedom from fear—which, translated into world terms, means a worldwide reduction of armaments to such a point and in such a thorough fashion that no nation will be in a position to commit an act of physical aggression against any neighbor—anywhere in the world.

That is no vision of a distant millenium. It is a definite basis for a kind of world attainable in our own time and generation. That kind of world is the very antithesis of the so-called new order of tyranny which the dictators seek to create with the crash of a bomb.

To that new order we oppose the greater conception—the moral order. A good society is able to face schemes of world domination and foreign revolutions alike without fear.

Since the beginning of our American history we have been engaged in change—in a perpetual peaceful revolution—a revolution which goes on steadily, quietly adjusting itself to changing conditions—without the concentration camp or the quick-lime in the ditch. The world order which we seek is the cooperation of free countries, working together in a friendly, civilized society.

This nation has placed its destiny in the hands and heads and hearts of its millions of free men and women; and its faith in freedom under the guidance of God. Freedom means the supremacy of human rights everywhere. Our support goes to those who struggle to gain those rights or keep them. Our strength is in our unity of purpose.

To that high concept there can be no end save victory.

[From *The Public Papers and Addresses of Franklin D. Roosevelt* (New York: Macmillan, 1940), 9:663*ff*]

Questions for Reflection

What actions did Roosevelt ask of the United States or other powers in his 1937 Quarantine Speech? What actions *seemed* to be *implied*? Why do you think this speech caused a great outcry of opposition from those groups who did not want the United States to become involved in the affairs of other nations?

What, specifically, did Roosevelt propose that the United States do, in his 1941 speech? Was Roosevelt able to stake out a position between isolation and intervention? How would you assess his leadership in this crisis?

ANSWERS TO MULTIPLE-CHOICE AND TRUE-FALSE QUESTIONS

Multiple-Choice Questions

1-D, 2-D, 3-C, 4-A, 5-C, 6-D, 7-A, 8-D

True-False Questions

1-F, 2-F, 3-F, 4-T, 5-T, 6-F, 7-F, 8-F

29

THE WORLD AT WAR

CHAPTER OBJECTIVES

After you complete the reading and study of this chapter you should be able to

1. Describe the major military strategies in both the European and Pacific theaters.
2. Explain the problems relating to mobilization and financing of the war.
3. Describe the impact of the war on the economy.
4. Assess the impact of the war on women, blacks, and Japanese-Americans.
5. Explain the decisions made at the Yalta Conference.
6. Account for the decision to use the atomic bomb and discuss its consequences.

CHAPTER OUTLINE

I. America's early battles
  A. Retreat in the Pacific
    1. Collapse along the Pacific
    2. Surrender of the Philippines
    3. Japanese strategy
    4. Battle of the Coral Sea (May 1942)
  B. Midway: a turning point
  C. Early setbacks in the Atlantic
    1. Devastation from German submarines
    2. Strategy of small patrol vessels

II. Mobilization at home
  A. Preparedness and mobilization
  B. Economic conversion to war
    1. War Production Board
    2. Role of the Office of Scientific Research and Development
    3. Effects of wartime spending
  C. Financing the war
    1. Roosevelt's effort to raise taxes
    2. Congressional reaction to taxation
    3. Sale of bonds
  D. Impact of the war on the economy
    1. Personal incomes
    2. Efforts to control prices
    3. Efforts to control wages and farm prices
    4. Seizure of industries
  E. Social effects of the war on women
    1. Women in the civilian workforce and the military
    2. Changing attitudes toward sex roles
  F. Social effects of the war on blacks
    1. Problems of the segregated armed forces
    2. Role of blacks in war industries
      a. The March on Washington Movement
      b. Impact of black militancy
    3. Challenges to other forms of discrimination
    4. Militant white counterreaction
  G. Impact of the war on Japanese-Americans

1. General record of the war on civil
   liberties
2. Internment
H. Evidences of domestic conservatism
   1. Congressional elections of 1942
   2. Abolition of New Deal agencies
   3. Actions against labor
I. Congressional reaction to the war

III. The war in Europe
  A. Initial decisions
    1. Basis for moving against Germany
       first
    2. Aspects of joint conduct of the war
    3. The formulation of the decision for
       the North African invasion
  B. The North Africa campaign
  C. Agreements at Casablanca
  D. Sicily and Italy
    1. Invasion of Sicily
    2. Italian surrender
    3. German control of northern Italy
    4. The battle for Rome
  E. Strategic bombing of Europe
    1. British and American cooperation
    2. Impact of the bombing
  F. Decisions of the Teheran Conference
  G. The D-Day invasion
    1. Development and implementation
       of "Overlord"
    2. German reaction
    3. Invasion of the French
       Mediterranean coast
    4. Slowing momentum of the drive
       on Germany

IV. The war in the Pacific
  A. Guadalcanal offensive
  B. MacArthur's sweep up the West
     Pacific

1. Approval for the MacArthur plan
2. The technique of "leapfrogging"
C. Nimitz's moves in the Central Pacific
D. The naval battle of Leyte Gulf

V. The election of 1944
  A. Republican strategy
  B. Democratic vice-presidential choice
  C. Campaign and results

VI. Closing on Germany
  A. The German counteroffensive
  B. Allied moves

VII. The Yalta Conference
  A. Nature of the decisions
  B. Call for a United Nations
  C. Occupation of Germany
  D. Decisions about eastern Europe
  E. An assessment of the Yalta decisions

VIII. Collapse of the Third Reich
  A. Roosevelt's death
  B. Collapse of Germany
  C. Discovery of the Nazi Holocaust

IX. The grinding war in the Pacific
  A. Japanese resistance in the Philippines
  B. Occupation of Iwo Jima and Okinawa
  C. Impact of these victories on the
     conduct of the war

X. The atomic bomb
  A. Manhattan Project
  B. The decision to use the bomb
  C. Effect of dropping two bombs
  D. Negotiation for surrender

XI. The final ledger of the war
  A. Estimates of death and destruction
  B. Impact on the United States and the
     USSR

KEY ITEMS OF CHRONOLOGY

Battle of Midway	June 1942
American troops invade North Africa	November 1942
Casablanca Conference	January 1943
Teheran Conference	November– December 1943
Smith v. Allwright	1944
D-Day invasion	June 6, 1944
Yalta Conference	February 1945

Roosevelt's death and Truman's accession   April 12, 1945
V-E Day   May 8, 1945
Potsdam Conference   July 1945
Atomic bomb dropped on Hiroshima   August 6, 1945
Japan's surrender   September 2, 1945

TERMS TO MASTER

Listed below are some important terms or people with which you should be familiar after you complete the study of this chapter. Explain the significance of each name or term.

1. War Production Board
2. Office of Price Administration
3. rationing
4. "Rosie the Riveter"
5. *Smith v. Allwright*
6. War Relocation Camps
7. Smith-Connally Act
8. Winston Churchill
9. second front
10. unconditional surrender
11. General Dwight D. Eisenhower
12. Operation "Overlord"
13. "leapfrogging"
14. General Douglas MacArthur
15. Battle of Leyte Gulf
16. Yalta Conference
17. Nazi Holocaust
18. Hiroshima

VOCABULARY BUILDING

Listed below are some words used in this chapter. Look up each word in your dictionary.

1. seismic
2. cryptanalysts
3. watershed
4. vexations
5. pincers
6. strategic
7. expedite
8. holocaust
9. latent
10. labyrinth

EXERCISES FOR UNDERSTANDING

When you have completed reading the chapter, answer each of the following questions. If you have difficulty, go back and reread the section of the chapter related to the question.

Multiple-Choice Questions

Select the letter of the response that best completes the statement.

1. The Battle of Midway was the turning point of the war in the Pacific because that battle
   A. stopped the eastward advance of the Japanese.
   B. destroyed most of what was left of the American fleet after Pearl Harbor.
   C. destroyed the Japanese fleet so that they were unable to pursue naval war after this.
   D. placed the United States Air Force close enough to the mainland of Japan to carry out bombing raids there.

2. The wartime powers of the federal government expanded to include
   A. control of wages and prices.
   B. rationing of scarce materials.
   C. seizure of some businesses.
   D. all of the above

3. Blacks during World War II achieved
   A. an end to segregation in the military.
   B. equal employment opportunities in the government and industry.
   C. a court ruling outlawing white primaries.
   D. social and political equality in the South.

4. From the start, British and American leaders completely agreed

A. to defeat Japan first.
B. to attack Germany only indirectly through Africa.
C. to strike directly at Germany across the English Channel.
D. on none of the above

5. Strategic bombing of Germany in 1943
   A. cut German production by at least 25 percent.
   B. broke German morale.
   C. involved British and American planes.
   D. failed because of a lack of planes.

6. The Battle of Leyte Gulf was
   A. a prime example of the "leapfrogging" strategy.
   B. the largest naval battle in history.
   C. the Allies' worst defeat in the Pacific.
   D. the key to Allied success in Sicily and Italy.

7. The decisions made at the Yalta Conference did *not* include agreement that
   A. Russia would have three votes in the U.N. General Assembly.
   B. Russia would have an occupation zone in the nonindustrialized area of East Germany as well as in part of Berlin.
   C. free elections would be held in Poland to select a government.
   D. both Russia and the United States would reduce their armaments by half after the war ended.

8. American officials were slow to aid Jewish refugees because
   A. they feared anti-Semitism in the United States.
   B. their experience with wartime propaganda created doubts about reports of the Holocaust.
   C. reported evidence of genocide seemed beyond belief.
   D. all of the above

True-False Questions

Indicate whether each statement is true or false.

1. In the first half of 1942 German submarines sank several hundred ships just off the U.S. coast.
2. To finance World War II, FDR preferred deficits instead of higher taxes.
3. During the war, most working women for the first time were married women.
4. During World War II, Congress readily renewed and extended such New Deal programs as the National Youth Administration.
5. FDR, Churchill, and Stalin first met together in Teheran in 1943.
6. The major matter of dispute in the Democratic convention of 1944 was the selection of a vice-presidential nominee.
7. The War Refugee Board was amazingly successful at rescuing Jews from Europe.
8. The Manhattan Project developed the atomic bomb.

Essay Questions

1. Outline America's major strategy in the war against both Germany and Japan. Explain why this strategy was chosen.
2. What effects did World War II have on the power of the federal government? Be specific in your response.
3. Explain the major decisions made at Casablanca, Teheran, and Yalta.
4. How did the war affect the respective status of blacks, women, and Japanese-Americans?
5. What innovations, technical and tactical, helped the Allies win the war?
6. Russia continually called for a second front in Europe but the United States refused to oblige until June 1944. Why?

DOCUMENT

The Effects of the Atomic Bomb on Hiroshima

The United States military conducted extensive investigations of the effects the atomic bomb had on the populations of Hiroshima and Nagasaki. Excerpted here are selections from that survey. Note the physical destruction, the human casualties, and the effects on morale wrought by the bomb.

A single atomic bomb, the first weapon of its type ever used against a target, exploded over the city of Hiroshima at 0815 on the morning of 6 August 1945. Most of the industrial workers had already reported to work, but many workers were enroute and nearly all the school children and some industrial employees were at work in the open on the program of building removal to provide firebreaks and disperse valuables to the country. The attack came 45 minutes after the "all clear" had been sounded from a previous alert. Because of the lack of warning and the populace's indifference to small groups of planes, the explosion came as an almost complete surprise, and the people had not taken shelter. Many were caught in the open, and most of the rest in flimsily constructed homes or commercial establishments.

The bomb exploded slightly northwest of the center of the city. Because of this accuracy and the flat terrain and circular shape of the city, Hiroshima was uniformly and extensively devastated. Practically the entire densely or moderately built-up portion of the city was leveled by blast and swept by fire. A "fire-storm," a phenomenon which has occurred infrequently in other conflagrations, developed in Hiroshima: fires springing up almost simultaneously over the wide flat area around the center of the city drew in air from all directions. The inrush of air easily overcame the natural ground wind, which had a velocity of only about 5 miles per hour. The "fire-wind" attained a maximum velocity of 30 to 40 miles per hour 2 to 3 hours after the explosion. The "fire-wind" and the symmetry of the built-up center of the city gave a roughly circular shape to the 4.4 square miles which were almost completely burned out.

The surprise, the collapse of many buildings, and the conflagration contributed to an unprecedented casualty rate. Seventy to eighty thousand people were killed, or missing and presumed dead, and an equal number were injured. The magnitude of casualties is set in relief by a comparison with the Tokyo fire raid of 9–10 March 1945, in which, though nearly 16 square miles were destroyed, the number killed was no larger, and fewer people were injured.

The impact of the atomic bomb shattered the normal fabric of community life and disrupted the organizations for handling the disaster. In the 30 percent of the population killed and the additional 30 percent seriously injured were included corresponding proportions of the civil authorities and rescue groups. A mass flight from the city took place, as persons sought safety from the conflagration and a place for shelter and food. Within 24 hours, however, people were streaming back by the thousands in search of relatives and friends and to determine the extent of their property loss. Road blocks had to be set up along all routes leading into the city, to keep curious and unauthorized people out. The bulk of the dehoused population found refuge in the surrounding countryside; within the city the food supply was short and shelter virtually nonexistent. . . .

The status of medical facilities and personnel dramatically illustrates the difficulties facing authorities. Of more than 200 doctors in Hiroshima before the attack, over 90 percent were casualties and only about 30 physicians were able to perform their normal duties a month after the raid. Out of 1,780 nurses, 1,654 were killed or injured. Though some stocks of supplies had been dispersed, many were destroyed. Only three out of 45 civilian hospitals could be used, and two large Army hospitals were rendered unusable. Those within 3,000 feet of ground zero were totally destroyed, and the mortality rate of the occupants was practically 100 percent.

1. *Casualties.*—The most striking result of the atomic bombs was the great numbers of casualties. The exact number of dead and injured will never be known because of the confusion after the explosions. Persons unaccounted for might have been burned beyond recognition in the falling buildings, disposed of in one of the mass cremations of the first week of recovery, or driven out of the city to die or recover without any record remaining. No sure count of even the preraid populations existed. . . . In this uncertain situation, estimates of casualties have generally ranged between 100,000 and 180,000 for Hiroshima, and between 50,000 and 100,000 for Nagasaki. The Survey believes the dead at Hiroshima to have been between 70,000 and 80,000, with an equal number injured; at Nagasaki over 35,000 dead and somewhat more than that injured seems the most plausible estimate.

Most of the immediate casualties did not differ from those caused by incendiary or high-explosive raids. The outstanding difference was the presence of radiation effects, which became unmistakable about a week after the bombing. At the time of impact, however, the causes of death and injury were flash burns, secondary effects of blast and falling debris, and burns from blazing buildings. . . .

The seriousness of . . . radiation effects may be measured by the fact that 95 percent of the traced survivors of the immediate explosion who were within 3,000 feet suffered from radiation disease. . . .

. . . Some of the dead were said by survivors to have had their abdomens ruptured and intestines protruding; others were reported to have protruding eyes and tongues, and to have looked as if they had drowned. Thorough check by Allied investigators discredited these stories as evidence of direct blast effects; the normal effects of blast are internal hemorrhage and crushing. These external signs point to injuries from debris rather than blast.

Injuries produced by falling and flying debris were much more numerous, and naturally increased in number and seriousness nearer the center of the affected area. . . . There is no doubt that the bomb was the most important influence among the people of these areas in making them think that defeat was inevitable. . . .

Admiration for the bomb was more frequently expressed than anger. Over one-fourth of the people in the target cities and surrounding area said they were impressed by its power and by the scientific skill which underlay its discovery and production.

... The two raids were all-Japan events and were intended so: The Allied Powers were trying to break the fighting spirit of the Japanese people and their leaders, not just of the residents of Hiroshima and Nagasaki. ...

The reactions found in the bombed cities appeared in the country as a whole—fear and terror, anger and hatred against the users, admiration for the scientific achievement—though in each case with less intensity.

[The United States Strategic Bombing Survey, *The Effects of Atomic Bombs on Hiroshima and Nagasaki* (Washington, D.C.: U.S. Government Printing Office, 1946), pp. 3, 6, 15, 17–18, 21]

Questions for Reflection

How do you react to reading about the physical and human destruction wrought by the bomb? How do the reactions of the Japanese people to the impact of the bomb compare with what you would have expected their reactions to have been? How would you compare the use of the atomic bomb to the use of conventional weapons in war? What has been the legacy of Hiroshima and Nagasaki?

ANSWERS TO MULTIPLE-CHOICE AND TRUE-FALSE QUESTIONS

Multiple-Choice Questions

1-A, 2-D, 3-C, 4-D, 5-C, 6-B, 7-D, 8-D

True-False Questions

1-T, 2-F, 3-T, 4-F, 5-T, 6-T, 7-F, 8-T

30

THE FAIR DEAL AND CONTAINMENT

CHAPTER OBJECTIVES

After you complete the reading and study of this chapter you should be able to

1. Analyze the problems of demobilization and conversion to peacetime production.
2. Account for Truman's troubles with Congress and assess the measure of accomplishment that he achieved.
3. Explain the policy of containment and trace its development to 1950.
4. Account for Truman's reelection in 1948.
5. Assess the strength of McCarthyism in the United States.
6. Explain the origins of the Korean War and trace its major developments.

CHAPTER OUTLINE

I. Demobilization under Truman
  A. The Truman style
    1. Truman's background and character
    2. Domestic proposals of 1945
  B. Demobilization
    1. Rapid reduction of armed forces
    2. Escalation of birth rate
    3. Efforts for economic stabilization
  C. Efforts to control inflation
    1. Demands for wage increases
    2. A wave of strikes

    3. Truman's response to strikes
    4. Efforts to control prices
    5. The end of controls
  D. Congressional elections of 1946

II. Record of the Republican Congress
  A. Taft-Hartley Act
  B. Efforts for tax reduction
  C. Governmental reorganization
    1. Features of the National Security Act
    2. Changes in presidential succession
    3. Twenty-second Amendment

III. Development of the Cold War
  A. Creating the United Nations
    1. Background to the U.N.
    2. Scheme of its operations
    3. U.S. ratification of U.N. membership
  B. Differences with the Soviets
    1. Problems relating to eastern Europe
    2. Development of the peace treaties
    3. Proposals to control atomic energy
  C. Development of the containment policy
    1. Kennan's theory
    2. Problems in Iran, Turkey, and Greece
    3. The Truman Doctrine
    4. Greek-Turkish Aid
    5. The Marshall Plan
      a. The proposal
      b. European response

6. Division of Germany
   a. Merger of Allied zones
   b. Berlin Blockade
   c. Berlin Airlift
   d. Creation of West and East Germany
7. Development of NATO
8. Establishment of Israel

IV. Truman's domestic politics
   A. Democratic divisions
   B. Truman's game plan
   C. Efforts for civil rights for blacks
   D. The 1948 election
      1. The Republican position
      2. Democratic battle over civil rights
      3. Creation of the Dixiecrats
      4. Wallace's Progressive party
      5. Nature of the campaign
      6. Election results
      7. Assessment of the results
   E. The fate of the Fair Deal

V. The Cold War heats up
   A. Point Four Program
   B. China's fall to communism
      1. History of the movement in China
      2. Assessment of the Communist victory
   C. Soviet atomic bomb

D. Work on the hydrogen bomb
E. Decision to maintain peacetime military force

VI. The Korean War
   A. Background to conflict
   B. Response to the invasion
   C. Military developments
      1. Rout of the U.N. forces
      2. Counterattack
      3. The decision to invade the North
      4. Entry of the Chinese Communists
   D. The dismissal of MacArthur
      1. Reasons for the action
      2. Reactions to the firing
   E. Negotiations for peace

VII. Another red scare
   A. Evidences of espionage
   B. The Truman loyalty program
   C. The Alger Hiss case
   D. Conviction of spies
   E. McCarthy's witch-hunt
      1. The emergence of Senator McCarthy
      2. Assessment of his tactics
   F. The McCarran Internal Security Act

VIII. Assessing the Cold War

KEY ITEMS OF CHRONOLOGY

FDR dies	April 12, 1945
Taft-Hartley Act	1947
Truman Doctrine	1947
Marshall Plan launched	1947
Berlin Blockade and Berlin Airlift	June 1948–May 1949
Creation of Israel	1948
Hiss case	1948–1950
Establishment of NATO	April 1949
China became communist	1949
Senator Joseph McCarthy's speech in Wheeling, West Virginia, citing communists in the State Department	February 1950
Korean War	June 1950–July 1953
MacArthur dismissed	April 1951

TERMS TO MASTER

Listed below are some important terms or people with which you should be familiar after you complete the study of this chapter. Explain the significance of each name or term.

1. Servicemen's Readjustment Act
2. Henry A. Wallace
3. Taft-Hartley Act
4. National Security Act, 1947
5. CIA
6. Twenty-second Amendment
7. United Nations
8. "iron curtain"
9. George F. Kennan
10. containment
11. Truman Doctrine
12. Cold War
13. Marshall Plan
14. Berlin Blockade
15. NATO
16. Dixiecrats
17. Fair Deal
18. Douglas MacArthur
19. Alger Hiss
20. Joseph R. McCarthy
21. McCarran Act

VOCABULARY BUILDING

Listed below are some words used in this chapter. Look up each word in your dictionary.

1. credence
2. bipartisan
3. *realpolitik*
4. reparations
5. brandish
6. charnel
7. partition
8. intractable
9. censure
10. ploy

EXERCISES FOR UNDERSTANDING

When you have completed reading the chapter, answer each of the following questions. If you have difficulty, go back and reread the section of the chapter related to the question.

Multiple-Choice Questions

Select the letter of the response that best completes the statement.

1. Enacted in 1944, the G.I. Bill of Rights
   A. guaranteed constitutional rights to soldiers.
   B. organized postwar demobilization.
   C. provided federal funds for veterans' education, job training, and housing.
   D. established standard procedures for the Allies prior to the Normandy invasion.

2. After World War II, the American economy
   A. never reverted to peacetime production because of the Cold War.
   B. suffered from some inflation.
   C. plunged into a depression.
   D. maintained wage and price controls for more than eight years.

3. Congress passed *over Truman's veto*
   A. the Marshall Plan.
   B. the Taft-Hartley Act.
   C. the Twenty-second Amendment.
   D. all of the above

4. Postwar disagreements between the United States and the Soviet Union especially concerned
   A. the formation of the United Nations.
   B. governments in eastern Europe.
   C. the reconstruction of Japan.
   D. the Nuremberg trials.

5. The Marshall Plan was designed to
   A. help western European nations rebuild their armies.
   B. subvert communist nations into the capitalist camp.
   C. lend money to Western European nations.
   D. help all European nations, including communist ones, to rebuild their war-torn economies.

6. An important new issue in the 1948 presidential election was
   A. civil rights.
   B. organized labor.
   C. agricultural policy.
   D. the regulation of business.

7. Alger Hiss was convicted of
   A. belonging to the Communist party.
   B. passing atomic secrets to the Soviets.
   C. lying under oath.
   D. nothing—he was acquitted.

8. After 1950, the leader of the red scare was
   A. Richard Nixon.
   B. Owen Lattimore.
   C. Alger Hiss.
   D. Joseph McCarthy.

True-False Questions

Indicate whether each statement is true or false.

1. Harry S. Truman ended most New Deal programs.
2. The Taft-Hartley Act outlawed unions at any plant that paid at least the minimum wage.
3. The National Security Act of 1947 created the Central Intelligence Agency.
4. Aid to Greece and Turkey came before the Marshall Plan.

5. The new state of Israel was created by formal action of the U.N. General Assembly.
6. The Dixiecrat candidate in 1948 was Henry A. Wallace.
7. The communists gained control of China, the Soviets exploded an atomic device, and the Korean War started—all in 1949.
8. More than a dozen countries sent troops to fight alongside Americans in Korea.

Essay Questions

1. How successful was President Truman in achieving his domestic goals?
2. Account for the onset of the Cold War.
3. Compare and contrast the aid provided under the Truman Doctrine and under the Marshall Plan.
4. Why was Harry Truman reelected in 1948?
5. Was America's entry into the Korean War a success? Explain.
6. Why did Truman fire MacArthur? Was his action justified? What reactions did it bring?
7. What was the basis for Joe McCarthy's appeal to the American people? Assess the importance of his anticommunist crusade.

READINGS

Reading 1. Arthur Schlesinger Explains the Origins of the Cold War

The origin of the Cold War is one of today's complex and controversial historiographical problems. The issues involve which side was responsible for the hostility that developed after World War II between the United States and the Soviet Union. In the article excerpted here, Arthur M. Schlesinger, Jr., a prominent historian and adviser to President Kennedy, takes a position somewhat more centrist than that of the revisionists who place the blame for the Cold War on the United States. Writing in 1967 just after he had broken with the Johnson administration over the Vietnam War, Schlesinger here attempts to show just how complex the development of the Cold War was.

The orthodox American view, as originally set forth by the American government and as reaffirmed until recently by most American scholars, has been that the Cold War was the brave and essential response of free men to communist aggression. Some have gone back well before the Second World War to lay open the sources of Russian expansionism. Geopoliticians traced the Cold War to imperial Russian strategic ambitions which in the nineteenth century led to the Crimean War, to Russian penetration of the Balkans and the Middle East and to Russian pressure on Britain's "lifeline" to India. Ideologists traced it to the Communist Manifesto of 1848 ("the violent overthrow of the bourgeoisie lays the foundation for the sway of the proletariat"). Thoughtful observers (a phrase meant to exclude those who speak in Dullese about the unlimited evil of godless, atheistic, militant communism) concluded that classical Russian imperialism and Pan-Slavism, compounded after 1917 by Leninist messianism, confronted the West at the end of the Second World War with an inexorable drive for domination.

The revisionist thesis is very different. In its extreme form, it is that, after the death of Franklin Roosevelt and the end of the Second World War, the United States deliberately abandoned the wartime policy of collaboration and, exhilarated by the possession of the atomic bomb, undertook a course of aggression of its own designed to expel all Russian influence from Eastern Europe and to establish democratic-capitalist states on the very border of the Soviet Union. As the revisionists see it, this radically new American policy—or rather this resumption by Truman of the pre-Roosevelt policy of insensate anti-communism—left Moscow no alternative but to take measures in defense of its own borders. The result was the Cold War. . . .

. . . Any honest reappraisal of the origins of the Cold War requires the imaginative leap—which should in any case be as instinctive for the historian as it is prudent for the statesman—into the adversary's viewpoint. We must strive to see how, given Soviet perspectives, the Russians might conceivably have misread our signals, as we must reconsider how intelligently we read theirs.

Nor can the historian forget the conditions under which decisions are made, especially in a time like the Second World War. These were tired, overworked, aging men: in 1945, Churchill was 71 years old, Stalin had governed his country for 17 exacting years, Roosevelt his for 12 years nearly as exacting. . . . All—even Stalin, behind his screen of ideology—had become addicts of improvisation, relying on authority and virtuosity to conceal the fact that they were constantly surprised by developments. . . . None showed great tactical consistency, or cared much about it; all employed a certain ambiguity to preserve their power to decide big issues; and it is hard to know how to interpret anything any one of them said on any specific occasion. . . .

Peacemaking after the Second World War was not so much a tapestry as it was a hopelessly raveled and knotted mess of yarn. Yet, for purposes of clarity, it is essential to follow certain threads. One theme indispensable to an understanding of the Cold War is the contrast between two clashing views of world order: the "universalist" view, by which all nations shared a common interest in all the affairs of the world, and the "sphere-of-influence" view, by which each great power would be assured by the other great powers of an acknowledged predominance in its own area of special interest. The universalist view assumed that national security would be guaranteed by an international organization. The sphere-of-interest view assumed that national security would be guaranteed by the balance of power. While in practice these views have by no means been incompatible (indeed, our shaky peace has been based on a combination of the two), in the abstract they involved sharp contradictions.

The tradition of American thought in these matters was universalist. . . .

The Kremlin, on the other hand, thought *only* of spheres of interest; above all, the Russians were determined to protect their frontiers, and especially their border to the west, crossed so often and so bloodily in the dark course of their history. . . .

It is now pertinent to inquire why the United States rejected the idea of stabilizing the world by division into spheres of influence and insisted on an East European strategy. . . .

The first reason is that they regarded this solution as containing within itself the seeds of a third world war. The balance-of-power idea seemed inherently unstable. . . .

. . . the second objection: that the sphere-of-influence approach would, in the words of the State Department in 1945, "militate against the establishment and effective functioning of a broader system of general security in which all countries will have their part." The United Nations, in short, was seen as the alternative to the balance of power. . . .

Third, the universalists feared that the sphere-of-interest approach would be what Hull termed "a haven for the isolationists," who would advocate America's participation in Western Hemisphere affairs on condition that it did not participate in European or Asian affairs. . . .

Fourth, the sphere-of-interest solution meant the betrayal of the principles for which the Second World War was being fought—the Atlantic Charter, the Four Freedoms, the Declaration of the United Nations. . . .

Fifth, the sphere-of-influence solution would create difficult domestic problems in American politics. Roosevelt was aware of the six million or more Polish votes in the 1944 election. . . .

Sixth, if the Russians were allowed to overrun Eastern Europe without argument, would that satisfy them? . . .

But the great omission of the revisionists—and also the fundamental explanation of the speed with which the Cold War escalated—lies precisely in the fact that the Soviet Union was not a traditional national state. The Soviet Union was a phenomenon very different from America or Britain: it was a totalitarian state, endowed with an all-explanatory, all-consuming ideology, committed to the infallibility of government and party, still in a somewhat messianic mood, equating dissent with treason, and ruled by a dictator who, for all his quite extraordinary abilities, had his paranoid moments.

Marxism-Leninism gave the Russian leaders a view of the world according to which all societies were inexorably destined to proceed along appointed roads by appointed stages until they achieved the classless nirvana. . . .

A revisionist fallacy has been to treat Stalin as just another Realpolitik statesman, as Second World War revisionists see Hitler as just another Stresemann or Bismarck. But the record makes it clear that in the end nothing could satisfy Stalin's paranoia. His own associates failed. Why does anyone suppose that any conceivable American policy would have succeeded?

The difference between America and Russia in 1945 was that some Americans fundamentally believed that, over a long run, a modus vivendi with Russia was possible; while the Russians, so far as one can tell, believed in no more than a short-run modus vivendi with the United States.

In retrospect, if it is impossible to see the Cold War as a case of American aggression and Russian response, it is also hard to see it as a pure case of Russian aggression and American response. . . .

The Cold War could have been avoided only if the Soviet Union had not been possessed by convictions both of the infallibility of the communist word and of the inevitability of a communist world. These convictions turned an impasse between national states into a religious war, a tragedy of ability into one of necessity. One might wish that America had preserved the poise and proportion of the first years of the Cold War and had not succumbed to its own forms of self-righteousness. But the most rational American policies could hardly have averted the Cold War. Only if Russia began to recede from its messianic mission and to accept, in fact if not yet in principle, the permanence of the world of diversity, only then did the hope flicker that this long, dreary, costly contest may at last be taking forms less dramatic, less obsessive and less dangerous to the future kind.

[Arthur Schlesinger, Jr., "Origins of the Cold War," *Foreign Affairs* 46 (October 1967): 22–52]

Reading 2. Barton Bernstein Presents a Revisionist View

Barton Bernstein has been one of the leading revisionists in the controversy over the origins of the Cold War. The excerpt below will introduce the reader to the essentials of that view.

Despite some dissents, most American scholars have reached a general consensus on the origins of the Cold War. As confirmed internationalists who believe that Russia constituted a threat to America and its European allies after World War II, they have endorsed their nation's acceptance of its obligations as a world power in the forties and its desire to establish a world order of peace and prosperity. Convinced that only American efforts prevented the Soviet Union from expanding past Eastern Europe, they have generally praised the containment policies of the Truman Doctrine, the Marshall Plan, and NATO as evidence of America's acceptance of world responsibility. While chiding or condemning those on the right who opposed international involvement (or had even urged preventive war), they have also been deeply critical of those on the left who have believed that the Cold War could have been avoided, or that the United States shared substantial responsibility for the Cold War.

Despite the widespread acceptance of this interpretation, there has long been substantial evidence (and more recently a body of scholarship) which suggests that American policy was neither so innocent nor so nonideological; that American leaders sought to promote their conceptions of national interest and their values even at the conscious risk of provoking Russia's fears about her security. In 1945 these leaders apparently believed that American power would be adequate for the task of reshaping much of the world according to America's needs and standards.

By overextending policy and power and refusing to accept Soviet interests, American policy-makers contributed to the Cold War. There was little understanding of any need to restrain American political efforts and desires. Though it cannot be proved that the United States could have achieved a *modus vivendi* with the Soviet Union in these years there is evidence that Russian policies were reasonably cautious and conservative, and that there was at least a basis for accommodation. But this possibility slowly slipped away as President Harry S. Truman reversed Roosevelt's tactics of accommodation. As American demands for democratic governments in Eastern Europe became more vigorous, as the new administration delayed in providing economic assistance to Russia and in seeking international control of atomic energy, policy-makers met with increasing Soviet suspicion and antagonism. Concluding that Soviet-American cooperation was impossible, they came to believe that the Soviet state could be halted only by force or the threat of force. . . .

. . . It is clear that Truman was either incapable or unwilling to reexamine his earlier assumption (or decision) of using the bomb. Under the tutelage of Byrnes and Stimson, Truman had come to assume by July that the bomb should be used, and perhaps he was incapable of reconsidering this strategy because he found no compelling reason not to use the bomb. Or he may have consciously rejected the options because he wanted to use the bomb. Perhaps he was vindictive and wished to retaliate for Pearl Harbor and other atrocities. (In justifying the use of the bomb against the Japanese, he wrote a few days after Nagasaki, "The only language they seem to understand is the one we have been using to bombard them. When you have to deal with a beast you have to treat him as a beast.") Or, most likely, Truman agreed with Byrnes that using the bomb would advance other American policies: It would end the war before the Russians could gain a hold in Manchuria, it would permit the United States to exclude Russia from the occupation government of Japan, and it would make the Soviets more manageable in Eastern Europe. It would enable the United States to shape the peace according to its own standards.

At minimum, then, the use of the bomb reveals the moral insensitivity of the President—whether he used it because the moral implications did not compel a reexamination of assumptions, or because he sought retribution, or because he sought to keep Russia out of Manchuria and the occupation government of Japan, and to make her more manageable in Eastern Europe. In 1945 American foreign policy was not innocent, nor was it unconcerned about Russian power, nor did it assume that the United States lacked the power to impose its will on the Russian state, nor was it characterized by high moral purpose or consistent dedication to humanitarian principles.

While the Soviet Union would not generally permit in Eastern Europe conditions that conformed to Western ideals, Stalin was pursuing a cautious policy and seeking accommodation with the West. He was willing to allow capitalism but was suspicious of American efforts at economic penetration which could lead to political dominance. Though by the autumn of 1945 the governments in Russia's general area of influence were subservient in foreign policy, they varied in form and in degree of independence—democracy in Czechoslovakia (the only country in this area with a democratic tradition), free elections and the overthrow of the Communist party in Hungary, a Communist-formed coalition government in Bulgaria, a broadly based but Communist-dominated government in Poland, and a Soviet-imposed government in Rumania (the most anti-Russian of these nations). In all of these countries Communists controlled the ministries of interior (the police) and were able to suppress anti-Soviet groups, including anti-communist democrats.

Those who have attributed to Russia a policy of inexorable expansion have often neglected this immediate postwar period, or they have interpreted it simply as a necessary preliminary (a cunning strategy to allay American suspicions until the American Army demobilized and left the continent) to the consolidation and extension of power in east-central Europe. From this perspective, however, much of Stalin's behavior becomes strangely contradictory and potentially self-defeating. If he had planned to create puppets rather than an area of "friendly governments," why (as Isaac Deutscher asks) did Stalin "so stubbornly refuse to make any concessions to the Poles over their eastern frontiers"? Certainly, also, his demand for reparations from Hungary, Rumania, and Bulgaria would have been unnecessary if he had planned to take over these countries. (America's insistence upon using a loan to Russia to achieve political goals, and nearly twenty-month delay after Russia first submitted a specific proposal for assistance, led Harriman to suggest in November that the loan policy "may have contributed to their [Russian] avaricious policies in the countries occupied or liberated by the Red Army.")

Russian sources are closed, so it is not possible to prove that Soviet intentions were conservative; nor for the same reason is it possible for those who adhered to the thesis of inexorable Soviet expansion to prove their theory. But the available evidence better supports the thesis that these years should be viewed not as a cunning preliminary to the harshness of 1947 and afterward, but as an attempt to establish a *modus vivendi* with the West and to protect "socialism in one country." This interpretation explains more adequately why the Russians delayed nearly three years before ending dissent and hardening policies in the countries behind their own military lines. It would also explain why the Communist parties in France and Italy were cooperating with the coalition governments until these parties were forced out of the coalitions in 1947. . . .

If the Russian policy was conservative and sought accommodation (as now seems likely), then its failure must be explained by looking beyond Russian actions. Historians must reexamine this period and reconsider American policies. Were they directed toward compromise? Can they be judged as having sought adjustment? Or did they demand acquiescence to the American world view, thus thwarting real negotiations?

There is considerable evidence that American actions clearly changed after Roosevelt's death. Slowly abandoning the tactics of accommodation, they became even more vigorous after Hiroshima. The insistence upon rolling back Soviet influence in Eastern Europe, the reluctance to grant a loan for Russian reconstruction, the inability to reach an agreement on Germany, the maintenance of the nuclear monopoly—all of these could have contributed to the sense of Russian insecurity. The point, then, is that in 1945 and 1946 there may still have been possibilities for negotiations and settlements, for accommodations and adjustments, if the United States had been willing to recognize Soviet fears, to accept Soviet power in her areas of influence, and to ease anxieties.

[Barton J. Bernstein, "American Foreign Policy and the Origins of the Cold War," in *Politics and Policies of the Truman Administration*, edited by Barton J. Bernstein (Chicago: Quadrangle Books, 1970), pp. 15–49]

Questions for Reflection

After reading both excerpts and answering the questions that follow, attempt to write in a few paragraphs your own view of the origins of the Cold War.

What is the orthodox view of the origins of the Cold War? The revisionist view? What special considerations should be taken into account in attempting to explain the Cold War? What important theme does Schlesinger want the reader to consider in explaining the development of Cold War events? What does he think the revisionists have omitted in their analysis of the Cold War?

How does Bernstein's initial description of the consensus view of Cold War origins compare with Schlesinger's view above? Needless use of the atomic bomb is one of the central themes of revisionist history. How does Bernstein deal with this matter? How does he argue that the United States acted incorrectly in Eastern Europe? How do we know Russia's motives after World War II? What limitation does that place on historians?

ANSWERS TO MULTIPLE-CHOICE
AND TRUE-FALSE QUESTIONS

Multiple-Choice Questions

1-C, 2-B, 3-B, 4-B, 5-D, 6-A, 7-C, 8-D

True-False Questions

1-F, 2-F, 3-T, 4-T, 5-F, 6-F, 7-F, 8-T

31

THROUGH THE PICTURE WINDOW: SOCIETY AND CULTURE, 1945–1960

CHAPTER OBJECTIVES

After you complete the reading and study of this chapter you should be able to

1. Account for the emergence of a consumer culture in the prosperous postwar era.
2. Describe the growth of suburban America after World War II.
3. Illustrate the widespread conformity in American culture in the 1950s.
4. Understand the ideas of the major critics of conformity.
5. Explain the artistic and literary dissent beginning in the 1950s.

CHAPTER OUTLINE

I. Postwar economy
   A. Growth and prosperity
      1. Military spending
      2. International trade dominance
      3. Technological innovation
      4. "Baby boom" and consumer demand
   B. Consumer culture
      1. Television
      2. Marketing and packaging
      3. Credit cards
      4. Shopping malls
   C. Growth of suburbs
      1. Rural-to-urban migration
      2. Levittowns
      3. Automobiles and roads
      4. "White flight"

II. Postwar conformity
   A. Corporate life
      1. Large corporations
      2. Managerial personality
   B. Women and cult of domesticity
   C. Religion
      1. Growth in church membership
         a. Religious revival
         b. Patriotism
         c. Marketing of religion
      2. Reverend Norman Vincent Peale and "positive thinking"
      3. Neo-orthodoxy
         a. Critical of religiosity
         b. Reinhold Niebuhr

III. Social critics of conformity
   A. John Kenneth Galbraith's *The Affluent Society*
   B. John Keats's *The Crack in the Picture Window*
   C. David Riesman and *The Lonely Crowd*

IV. Alienation in the arts
  A. Drama
    1. Oppressiveness of mass culture
    2. Arthur Miller's *Death of a Salesman*
    3. Tennessee Williams and Edward Albee
  B. The novel
    1. The individual's struggle for survival
    2. J. D. Salinger's *Catcher in the Rye*
    3. *From Here to Eternity* by James Jones
    4. Saul Bellow, Ralph Ellison, Joseph Heller, Norman Mailer, Joyce Carol Oates, et al.
  C. Painting
    1. Edward Hopper and desolate loneliness
    2. Abstract expressionism
      a. Violent and chaotic modern society
      b. Jackson Pollock
      c. William de Kooning, Mark Rothko, et al.
  D. The Beats
    1. Liberation of self-expression
    2. Greenwich Village background
    3. William Burrough's *Naked Lunch*
    4. *Howl* by Allen Ginsberg
    5. Jack Kerouac's *On the Road*
    6. Influences

KEY ITEMS OF CHRONOLOGY

Dr. Benjamin Spock's *Common Sense Book of Baby and Child Care*	1946
The first Levittown in New York	1947
Arthur Miller's *Death of a Salesman*	1949
David Riesman's *The Lonely Crowd*	1950
J. D. Salinger's *Catcher in the Rye*	1951
"one Nation under God" added to the Pledge of Allegiance	1954
Allen Ginsberg's *Howl*	1956
Jack Kerouac's *On the Road*	1957
John Kenneth Galbraith's *The Affluent Society*	1958
Vance Packard's *The Waste Makers*	1960

TERMS TO MASTER

Listed below are some important terms or people with which you should be familiar after you complete the study of this chapter. Explain the significance of each name or term.

1. baby-boom generation
2. suburbs
3. William Levitt
4. "white flight"
5. white collar
6. cult of domesticity
7. "in God we trust"
8. Norman Vincent Peale
9. neo-orthodoxy
10. Reinhold Niebuhr
11. "other-directed"
12. *Death of a Salesman*
13. Holden Caulfield
14. abstract expressionism
15. Jackson Pollock
16. The Beats

VOCABULARY BUILDING

Listed below are some words used in this chapter. Look up each word in your dictionary.

1. prolific
2. wean
3. obsolescence
4. discretionary
5. orthodoxy
6. harangue
7. religiosity
8. inculcate
9. vaunted
10. stupefy
11. kaleidoscopic

EXERCISES FOR UNDERSTANDING

When you have completed reading the chapter, answer each of the following questions. If you have difficulty, go back and reread the section of the chapter related to the question.

Multiple-Choice Questions

Select the letter of the response that best completes the statement.

1. Nine out of ten American homes had a television set by
   A. 1940.
   B. 1950.
   C. 1960.
   D. 1970.

2. William Levitt was a leading
   A. suburban home builder.
   B. Beat poet.
   C. radio and television minister.
   D. critic of conformity in the 1950s.

3. The ideal for a middle-class woman in the 1950s was to be
   A. an independent white-collar professional.
   B. a wife and mother.
   C. employed outside the home.
   D. none of the above

4. The religious revival of the 1950s was spurred by

A. the Cold War.
B. television.
C. a mobile population's need for community.
D. all of the above

5. Norman Vincent Peale urged Americans to
   A. buy his homes in the suburbs.
   B. "stop worrying and start living."
   C. give up all worldly possessions.
   D. realize that pain was part of real peace.

6. John Keats's *The Crack in the Picture Window* was a stinging critique of
   A. the quality of housing in the suburbs.
   B. television.
   C. modern art.
   D. suburban life.

7. A leading abstract expressionist painter was
   A. Gregory Corso.
   B. Ralph Ellison.
   C. Jackson Pollock.
   D. Reinhold Niebuhr.

8. The Beats included
   A. Arthur Miller, Edward Albee, and Tennessee Williams.
   B. William de Kooning, Mark Rothko, and Robert Motherwell.
   C. William Burroughs, Allen Ginsburg, and Jack Kerouac.
   D. none of the above

True-False Questions

Indicate whether each statement is true or false.

1. Defense spending was the most important contributor to economic growth after World War II.
2. Consumer debt declined in the prosperous 1950s.
3. The baby boom began in the late 1950s.
4. "In God We Trust" was put on all American currency starting in 1955.
5. The leading exponent of "positive thinking" was Reinhold Niebuhr.
6. According to David Riesman, the "inner-directed" person lives according to a set of basic values similar to the Protestant work ethic.

7. The author of *Catcher in the Rye* was J. D. Salinger.
8. Allen Ginsberg's autobiography was *On the Road.*

Essay Questions

1. What factors contributed to the economic growth and prosperity of the postwar period?
2. Who was William Levitt and why was his work important?

3. Describe some of the drawbacks of suburban living in the 1950s.
4. Compare and contrast the ideas of Norman Vincent Peale and Reinhold Niebuhr.
5. How did many important postwar novels reinforce the image of Americans as "a lonely crowd"? Refer to specific examples.
6. Who were the Beats and what were their concerns?

DOCUMENT

Betty Friedan Describes the Attitude of the "Bored Housewife"

As the text shows, the ideal American woman in the 1950s was the housewife-mother. In the following excerpt from her influential work *The Feminine Mystique* (1963), Betty Friedan analyzes this "ideal" and explores how it came about.

In the early 1960's *McCall's* has been the fastest growing of the women's magazines. The image of woman that emerges from this big, pretty magazine is young and frivolous, almost childlike; fluffy and feminine; passive; gaily content in a world of bedroom and kitchen, sex, babies, and home. The magazine surely does not leave out sex; the only passion, the only pursuit, the only goal a woman is permitted is the pursuit of a man. It is crammed full of food, clothing, cosmetics, furniture, and the physical bodies of young women, but where is the world of thought and ideas, the life of the mind and spirit? In the magazine image, women do no work except housework and work to keep their bodies beautiful and to get and keep a man.

This was the image of the American woman in the year Castro led a revolution in Cuba and men were trained to travel into outer space; the year that the African continent brought forth new nations, and a plane whose speed is greater than the speed of sound broke up a Summit Conference; the year artists picketed a great museum in protest against the hegemony of abstract art; physicists explored the concept of anti-matter; astronomers, because of new radio telescopes, had to alter their concepts of the expanding universe; biologists made a breakthrough in the fundamental chemistry of life; and Negro youth in Southern schools forced the United States, for the first time since the Civil War, to face a moment of democratic truth. But this magazine, published for over 5,000,000 American women, almost all of whom have been through high school and nearly half to college, contained almost no mention of the world beyond the home. In the second half of the twentieth century in America, woman's world was confined to her own body and beauty, the charming of man, the bearing of babies, and the physical care and serving of husband, children, and home. And this was no anomaly of a single issue of a single women's magazine.

I sat one night at a meeting of magazine writers, mostly men, who work for all kinds of magazines, including women's magazines. . . . [We] spent an hour listening to Thurgood Marshall on the inside story of the desegregation battle, and its possible effect on the presidential election. "Too bad I can't run that story," one editor said. "But you just can't link it to woman's world."

As I listened to them, a German phrase echoed in my mind—*"Kinder, Kuche, Kirche,"* the slogan by which the Nazis decreed that women must once again be confined to their biological role. But this was not Nazi Germany. This was America. The whole world lies open to American women. Why, then, does the image deny the world? Why does it limit women to "one position, one role, one occupation"? Not long ago, women dreamed and fought for equality, their own place in the world. What happened to their dreams; when did women decide to give up the world and go back home?

I sat for many days in the New York Public Library, going back through bound volumes of American women's magazines for the last twenty years. I found a change in the image of the American woman, and in the boundaries of the woman's world, as sharp and puzzling as the changes revealed in the cores of ocean sediment.

In 1939, the heroines of women's magazine stories were not always young, but in a certain sense they were younger than their fictional counterparts today. They were young in the same way that the American hero has always been young: they were New Women, creating with a gay determined spirit a new identity for women—a life of their own. There was an aura about them of becoming, of moving into a future that was going to be different from the past. The majority of heroines in the four major women's magazines (then *Ladies' Home Journal, McCall's, Good Housekeeping, Woman's Home Companion*) were career women—happily, proudly, adventurously, attractively career women—who loved and were loved by men. And the spirit, courage, independence, determination—the strength of character they showed in their work as nurses, teachers, artists, actresses, copywriters, saleswomen—were part of their charm. There was a definite aura that their individuality was something to be admired, not unattractive to men, that men were drawn to them as much for their spirit and character as for their looks.

These were the mass women's magazines—in their heyday. The stories were conventional: girl-meets-boy or girl-gets-boy. But very often this was not the major theme of the story. These heroines were usually marching toward some goal or vision of their own, struggling with some problem of work or the world, when they found their man. And this New Woman, less fluffily feminine, so independent and determined to find a new life of her own, was the heroine of a different kind of love story. She was less aggressive in pursuit of a man. Her passionate involvement with the world, her own sense of herself as an individual, her self-reliance, gave a different flavor to her relationship with the man.

These stories may not have been great literature. But the identity of their heroines seemed to say something about the housewives who, then as now, read the women's magazines. These magazines

were not written for career women. The New Woman heroines
were the ideal of yesterday's housewives; they reflected the dreams,
mirrored the yearning for identity and the sense of possibility that
existed for women then. And if women could not have these dreams
for themselves, they wanted their daughters to have them. They
wanted their daughters to be more than housewives, to go out in the
world that had been denied them.

As for not earning any money, the argument goes, let the housewife
compute the cost of her services. Women can save more money by
their managerial talents inside the home than they can bring into
it by outside work. As for woman's spirit being broken by the bore-
dom of household tasks, maybe the genius of some women has been
thwarted, but "a world full of feminine genius, but poor in children,
would come rapidly to an end. . . . Great men have great mothers."

The feminine mystique says that the highest value and the only
commitment for women is the fulfillment of their own femininity.
It says that the great mistake of Western culture, through most of
its history, has been the undervaluation of this femininity. It says
this femininity is so mysterious and intuitive and close to the creation and origin of life that man-made science may never be able
to understand it. But however special and different, it is in no way
inferior to the nature of man; it may even in certain respects be
superior. The mistake, says the mystique, the root of women's troubles in the past is that women envied men, women tried to be like
men, instead of accepting their own nature, which can find fulfillment only in sexual passivity, male domination, and nurturing ma-
ternal love.

But the new image this mystique gives to American women is the
old image: "Occupation: housewife." The new mystique makes the
housewife-mothers, who never had a chance to be anything else,
the model for all women; it presupposes that history has reached a
final and glorious end in the here and now, as far as women are
concerned. Beneath the sophisticated trappings, it simply makes
certain concrete, finite, domestic aspects of feminine existence—as
it was lived by women whose lives were confined, by necessity, to
cooking, cleaning, washing, bearing children—into a religion, a pattern by which all women must now live or deny their femininity.

Fulfillment as a woman had only one definition for American
women after 1949—the housewife-mother. As swiftly as in a dream,
the image of the American woman as a changing, growing individual in a changing world was shattered. Her solo flight to find her
own identity was forgotten in the rush for the security of togetherness. Her limitless world shrunk to the cozy walls of home.

The end of the road, in an almost literal sense, is the disappearance
of the heroine altogether, as a separate self and the subject of her
own story. The end of the road is togetherness, where the woman
has no independent self to hide even in guilt; she exists only for and
through her husband and children.

Coined by the publishers of *McCall's* in 1954, the concept "togetherness" was seized upon avidly as a movement of spiritual
significance by advertisers, ministers, newspaper editors. For a
time, it was elevated into virtually a national purpose. But very

quickly there was sharp social criticism, and bitter jokes about "togetherness" as a substitute for larger human goals—for men. Women were taken to task for making their husbands do housework, instead of letting them pioneer in the nation and the world. Why, it was asked, should men with the capacities of statesmen, anthropologists, physicists, poets, have to wash dishes and diaper babies on weekday evenings or Saturday mornings when they might use those extra hours to fulfill larger commitments to their society?

But forbidden to join man in the world, can women be people? Forbidden independence, they finally are swallowed in an image of such passive dependence that they want men to make the decisions, even in the home. The frantic illusion that togetherness can impart a spiritual content to the dullness of domestic routine, the need for a religious movement to make up for the lack of identity, betrays the measure of women's loss and the emptiness of the image. Could making men share the housework compensate women for their loss of the world? Could vacuuming the living-room floor together give the housewife some mysterious new purpose in life?

In 1956, at the peak of togetherness, the bored editors of *McCall's* ran a little article called "The Mother Who Ran Away." To their amazement, it brought the highest readership of any article they had ever run. "It was our moment of truth," said a former editor. "We suddenly realized that all those women at home with their three and a half children were miserably unhappy."

But by then the new image of American woman, "Occupation: housewife," had hardened into a mystique, unquestioned and permitting no questions. . . .

By the time I started writing for women's magazines, in the fifties, it was simply taken for granted by editors, and accepted as an immutable fact of life by writers, that women were not interested in politics, life outside the United States, national issues, art, science, ideas, adventure, education, or even their own communities, except where they could be sold through their emotions as wives and mothers.

Politics, for women, became Mamie's clothes and the Nixons' home life. Out of conscience, a sense of duty, the *Ladies' Home Journal* might run a series like "Political Pilgrim's Progress," showing women trying to improve their children's schools and playgrounds. But even approaching politics through mother love did not really interest women, it was thought in the trade. Everyone knew those readership percentages. An editor of *Redbook* ingeniously tried to bring the bomb down to the feminine level by showing the emotions of a wife whose husband sailed into a contaminated area.

"Women can't take an idea, an issue, pure," men who edited the mass women's magazines agreed. "It had to be translated in terms they can understand as women." This was so well understood by those who wrote for women's magazines that a natural childbirth expert submitted an article to a leading woman's magazine called "How to Have a Baby in a Atom Bomb Shelter." "The article was not well written," an editor told me, "or we might have bought it."

According to the mystique, women, in their mysterious femininity, might be interested in the concrete biological details of having a baby in a bomb shelter, but never in the abstract idea of the bomb's power to destroy the human race.

Such a belief, of course, becomes a self-fulfilling prophecy. In 1960, a perceptive social psychologist showed me some sad statistics which seemed to prove unmistakably that American women under thirty-five are not interested in politics. "They may have the vote, but they don't dream about running for office," he told me. "If you write a political piece, they won't read it. You have to translate it into issues they can understand–romance, pregnancy, nursing, home furnishings, clothes. Run an article on the economy, or the race question, civil rights, and you'd think that women had never heard of them."

This is the real mystery: why did so many American women, with the ability and education to discover and create, go back home again, to look for "something more" in housework and rearing children? For, paradoxically, in the same fifteen years in which the spirited New Woman was replaced by the Happy Housewife, the boundaries of the human world have widened, the pace of world change has quickened, and the very nature of human reality has become increasingly free from biological and material necessity.

[From Betty Friedan, *The Feminine Mystique* (New York: W. W. Norton & Co., 1974; originally published 1963), pp. 36, 37, 38, 40, 42, 43–44, 47–48, 50–51, 67]

Questions for Reflection

What effects do the images depicted in magazines (and on television) have on readers (and viewers)? Discuss this with specific regard to the images of women in the 1950s. What does Friedan see as "the feminine mystique," and what does she think of it? How appropriate is "the feminine mystique" as a guideline for women today?

ANSWERS TO MULTIPLE-CHOICE AND TRUE-FALSE QUESTIONS

Multiple-Choice Questions

1-C, 2-A, 3-B, 4-D, 5-B, 6-D, 7-C, 8-C

True-False Questions

1-T, 2-F, 3-F, 4-T, 5-F, 6-T, 7-T, 8-F

32

CONFLICT AND DEADLOCK:
THE EISENHOWER YEARS

CHAPTER OBJECTIVES

After you complete the reading and study of this chapter you should be able to

1. Describe the Eisenhower style and his approach to the nation's problems.
2. Assess the nature of modern Republicanism in relation to New Deal liberalism, focusing especially on Eisenhower's stance on key domestic legislation.
3. Assess the early performance of Dulles's diplomacy, especially as compared to the policy of containment.
4. Explain the origins of the Indochina War and assess Eisenhower's response to it.
5. Describe the developments in civil rights in the Eisenhower era and assess his responses to them.
6. Explain the Suez Crisis and the Hungarian revolt, their interrelations and their consequences.
7. Assess the impact of Sputnik.

CHAPTER OUTLINE

I. Rise of Eisenhower
  A. Election of 1952
    1. Appeal of Ike
    2. Adlai Stevenson
  B. Ike's background and personality
    1. Army career
    2. Warm and unpretentious

II. The early Eisenhower administration
  A. Appointments
  B. Dynamic conservatism
    1. Some New Deal programs cut
      a. Reconstruction Finance Corporation
      b. Wage and price controls
    2. Some New Deal programs extended
      a. Social security
      b. Minimum wage
      c. Health care
      d. Housing
  C. Public works
    1. St. Lawrence Seaway
    2. Interstate highways
  D. Armistice in Korea
    1. Ike's bold stand
    2. Reasons for settlement
  E. End to McCarthyism
    1. McCarthy's tactics
    2. McCarthy and the army
    3. Senate condemnation
  F. Internal security worries
  G. Dulles and foreign policy
    1. Dulles's background

2. Idea of liberation
3. Covert action and Allen Dulles
4. Massive retaliation
5. Brinksmanship
H. Problems of Indochina
1. Background to war
   a. Nationalism in Asia
   b. French control
   c. Ho Chi Minh and independence
2. First Indochina war
   a. Outbreak of fighting
   b. American aid
   c. Ike's domino theory
3. Geneva Accords
   a. French defeat
   b. Provisions of the agreement
4. Creation of SEATO
5. Government of Diem
   a. Need for reform
   b. Opposition suppressed

III. Stirrings in civil rights
A. Ike's stance on civil rights
B. *Brown v. Board of Education*
1. Court's decision
2. Reactions
   a. Eisenhower's reluctance
   b. Token compliance
   c. Massive resistance
C. Montgomery bus boycott
1. Cause for action
2. Role of Martin Luther King, Jr.
3. Strategy of nonviolence
4. Results
D. Civil rights legislation
E. Little Rock

IV. Election of 1956
A. Eisenhower's health
B. Stevenson defeated again
V. A season of troubles
A. The Suez crisis
1. Eisenhower's Middle East policy
2. Rise of Nasser in Egypt
3. Offer and withdrawal of loan
4. Nasser's seizure of Suez
5. Israeli invasion
6. Resolution of crisis
B. The Hungarian revolt
C. Sputnik
1. The Russian feat
2. American reactions
   a. U.S. space effort
   b. Deployment of missiles
   c. Creation of NASA
   d. National Defense Education Act
D. Corruption in administration
E. Other foreign problems
1. Eisenhower doctrine
2. Marines to Lebanon
3. The Berlin problem
4. The U-2 affair
   a. Spy plane downed
   b. Collapse of summit
5. Castro's Cuba
   a. Castro's takeover
   b. American responses
VI. Assessing the Eisenhower years
A. Accomplishments
B. Farewell address

KEY ITEMS OF CHRONOLOGY

TERMS TO MASTER

Listed below are some important terms or people with which you should be familiar after you complete the study of this chapter. Explain the significance of each name or term.

1. Adlai Stevenson
2. "dynamic conservatism"
3. St. Lawrence Seaway
4. Interstate Highway System
5. Earl Warren
6. "liberation"
7. "massive retaliation"
8. Ho Chi Minh
9. Dien Bien Phu
10. Geneva Accords
11. SEATO
12. *Brown v. Board of Education*
13. Martin Luther King, Jr.
14. Suez crisis
15. Sputnik
16. U-2 incident

VOCABULARY BUILDING

Listed below are some words used in this chapter. Look up each word in your dictionary.

1. incumbent
2. egghead
3. syntax
4. renege
5. armistice
6. splenetic
7. capricious
8. sonorous
9. scurrilous
10. acclamation

EXERCISES FOR UNDERSTANDING

When you have completed reading the chapter, answer each of the following questions. If you have difficulty, go back and reread the section of the chapter related to the question.

Multiple-Choice Questions

Select the letter of the response that best completes the statement.

1. The Eisenhower administration
   A. reduced farm subsidies.
   B. extended Social Security benefits.
   C. started the Interstate Highway System.
   D. did all of the above

2. Senator McCarthy met his downfall as a result of a direct conflict with
   A. Eisenhower, whom he called a Communist.
   B. the FBI.
   C. the State Department.
   D. the United States Army.

3. Eisenhower once said the "biggest damnfool mistake I ever made" was
   A. retiring from the army and entering politics.
   B. appointing Earl Warren to the Supreme Court.
   C. not attacking China with atomic weapons.
   D. using federal troops in Little Rock, Arkansas.

4. The Geneva Accords involving Southeast Asia
   A. were signed by the United States.
   B. neutralized Vietnam.
   C. divided Laos and Cambodia at the 38th Parallel.
   D. called for elections to unify Vietnam.

5. In *Brown v. Board of Education,* the Supreme Court ruled that
   A. racial segregation was constitutional.
   B. "separate but equal" in public education was unconstitutional.
   C. all children under the age of eighteen had to attend school.
   D. Kansas must provide free education for Indian children.

6. The Civil Rights Act of 1957
   A. was supported by Eisenhower and Lyndon Johnson.
   B. established the Civil Rights Commission.
   C. focused on voting rights for blacks.
   D. did all of the above

7. In the Suez crisis of 1956, the United States was on the same side as
   A. the Soviet Union.
   B. France and Great Britain.
   C. Israel.
   D. Hungary.

8. Eisenhower's Farewell Address dealt with
   A. the need for greater military spending.
   B. the dangers of a military-industrial complex.
   C. how to solve problems of civil rights.
   D. the need for a better highway system.

True-False Questions

Indicate whether each statement is true or false.

1. Eisenhower's chief rival for the 1952 nomination was Senator Joseph McCarthy of Ohio.
2. The Eisenhower administration was especially strong in its denunciation of U.S. policy commitments made at Yalta.
3. Under Secretary of State Dulles, American policy radically changed from the containment followed by Truman and Acheson.
4. SEATO was exactly like NATO except in Southeast Asia.

5. Eisenhower thought that laws could quickly and easily provide equal rights for blacks.
6. The leader of the Montgomery bus boycott was Martin Luther King, Jr.
7. The NDEA was a United States response to the launching of Sputnik.
8. Eisenhower always worked with solid Republican majorities in Congress.

Essay Questions

1. How did Ike's administrative style, philosophy, and programs differ from those of the New Deal?
2. What factors contributed to the fall of Senator McCarthy?
3. How did the Eisenhower administration try to "contain" communism?
4. Assess America's involvement in Indochina during the Eisenhower administration.
5. Describe the first developments in the civil rights movement.
6. Account for the United States position in both the Suez crisis and the Hungarian revolt of 1956.
7. What was the U-2 and how did it affect American foreign policy?

DOCUMENT

Eisenhower's Farewell Address, January 17, 1961

Eisenhower's farewell address, below, includes his famous warning about the growing influence of "the military-industrial complex."

> *My fellow Americans:*
> Three days from now, after half a century in the service of our country, I shall lay down the responsibilities of office as, in traditional and solemn ceremony, the authority of the Presidency is vested in my successor. . . .
> We now stand ten years past the midpoint of a century that has witnessed four major wars among great nations. Three of them involved our own country. Despite these holocausts America is today the strongest, the most influential and most productive nation in the world. Understandably proud of this pre-eminence we yet

realize that America's leadership and prestige depend, not merely upon our unmatched material progress, riches and military strength, but on how we use our power in the interests of world peace and human betterment.

Throughout America's adventure in free government, our basic purposes have been to keep the peace; to foster progress in human achievement, and to enhance liberty, dignity and integrity among people and among nations. To strive for less would be unworthy of a free and religious people. Any failure traceable to arrogance, or our lack of comprehension or readiness to sacrifice would inflict upon us grievous hurt both at home and abroad.

Progress toward these noble goals is persistently threatened by the conflict now engulfing the world. It commands our whole attention, absorbs our very beings. We face a hostile ideology— global in scope, atheistic in character, ruthless in purpose, and insidious in method. Unhappily the danger it poses promises to be of indefinite duration. To meet it successfully, there is called for, not so much the emotional and transitory sacrifices of crisis, but rather those which enable us to carry forward steadily, surely, and without complaint the burdens of a prolonged and complex struggle— with liberty the stake. Only thus shall we remain, despite every provocation, on our charted course toward permanent peace and human betterment. . . .

A vital element in keeping the peace is our military establishment. Our arms must be mighty, ready for instant action, so that no potential aggressor may be tempted to risk his own destruction.

Our military organization today bears little relation to that known by any of my predecessors in peacetime, or indeed by the fighting men of World War II or Korea.

Until the latest of our world conflicts, the United States had no armaments industry. American makers of plowshares could, with time and as required, make swords as well. But now we can no longer risk emergency improvisation of national defense; we have been compelled to create a permanent armaments industry of vast proportions. Added to this, three and a half million men and women are directly engaged in the defense establishment. We annually spend on military security more than the net income of all United States corporations.

This conjunction of an immense military establishment and a large arms industry is new in the American experience. The total influence—economic, political, even spiritual—is felt in every city, every statehouse, every office of the federal government. We recognize the imperative need for this development. Yet we must not fail to comprehend its grave implications. Our toil, resources, and livelihood are all involved; so is the very structure of our society.

In the councils of government, we must guard against the acquisition of unwarranted influence, whether sought or unsought, by the military-industrial complex. The potential for the disastrous rise of misplaced power exists and will persist.

We must never let the weight of this combination endanger our liberties or democratic processes. We should take nothing for granted. Only an alert and knowledgeable citizenry can compel the proper meshing of the huge industrial and military machinery of

268 CHAPTER THIRTY-TWO

defense with our peaceful methods and goals, so that security and liberty may prosper together.

Akin to, and largely responsible for the sweeping changes in our industrial-military posture, has been the technological revolution during recent decades.

In this revolution, research has become central; it also becomes more formalized, complex, and costly. A steadily increasing share is conducted for, by, or at the direction of, the federal government. . . .

The prospect of domination of the nation's scholars by federal employment, project allocations, and the power of money is ever present—and is gravely to be regarded.

Yet, in holding scientific research and discovery in respect, as we should, we must also be alert to the equal and opposite danger that public policy could itself become the captive of a scientific-technological elite.

It is the task of statesmanship to mold, to balance, and to integrate these and other forces, new and old, within the principles of our democratic system—ever aiming toward the supreme goals of our free society.

Another factor in maintaining balance involves the element of time. As we peer into society's future, we—you and I, and our government—must avoid the impulse to live only for today, plundering, for our own ease and convenience, the precious resources of tomorrow. We cannot mortgage the material assets of our grandchildren without risking the loss also of their political and spiritual heritage. We want democracy to survive for all generations to come, not to become the insolvent phantom of tomorrow.

Down the long lane of the history yet to be written America knows that this world of ours, ever growing smaller, must avoid becoming a community of dreadful fear and hate, and be, instead, a proud confederation of mutual trust and respect.

Such a confederation must be one of equals. The weakest must come to the conference table with the same confidence as do we, protected as we are by our moral, economic, and military strength. That table, though scarred by many past frustrations, cannot be abandoned for the certain agony of the battlefield.

Disarmament, with mutual honor and confidence, is a continuing imperative. Together we must learn how to compose differences, not with arms, but with intellect and decent purpose. Because this need is so sharp and apparent I confess that I lay down my official responsibilities in this field with a definite sense of disappointment. As one who has witnessed the horror and the lingering sadness of war—as one who knows that another war could utterly destroy this civilization which has been so slowly and painfully built over thousands of years—I wish I could say tonight that a lasting peace is in sight.

Happily, I can say that war has been avoided. Steady progress toward our ultimate goal has been made. But, so much remains to be done. As a private citizen, I shall never cease to do what little I can to help the world advance along that road. . . .

[From *Public Papers of the Presidents: Dwight D. Eisenhower,* 1960–1961 (Washington, D. C.: U. S. Government Printing Office, 1961), no. 421, pp. 1035–1040]

Questions for Reflection

Describe the conflict that Eisenhower sees as "now engulfing the world." Why does Eisenhower consider it significant that the United States for the first time had a permanent armaments industry? What dangers does he think the "military-industrial complex" poses? Explain whether or not you agree with Eisenhower's analysis.

ANSWERS TO MULTIPLE-CHOICE AND TRUE-FALSE QUESTIONS

Multiple-Choice Questions

1-D, 2-D, 3-B, 4-D, 5-B, 6-D, 7-A, 8-B

True-False Questions

1-F, 2-F, 3-F, 4-F, 5-F, 6-T, 7-T, 8-F

33

NEW FRONTIERS:
KENNEDY AND JOHNSON

CHAPTER OBJECTIVES

After you complete the reading and study of this chapter you should be able to

1. Describe Kennedy's style and compare it to the style of his predecessor and successor.
2. Assess Kennedy's domestic legislative achievements.
3. Assess the Kennedy record in foreign affairs.
4. Describe and account for LBJ's legislative accomplishments.
5. Explain why the Vietnam War became a quagmire for the United States and why LBJ changed his policy there in 1968.
6. Trace the transformation of the civil rights movement into the black power movement.

CHAPTER OUTLINE

I. The 1960 election
   A. Nixon's experience
   B. Kennedy's background
   C. Campaign
      1. Televised debates
      2. Results

II. The New Frontier
   A. Start of the administration
      1. Appointments
      2. Inaugural address
   B. Legislative achievements
      1. Urban renewal, minimum wage, social security
      2. Alliance for Progress
      3. Peace Corps
      4. Trade Expansion Act
   C. Civil rights
      1. Kennedy's commitment
      2. Martin Luther King, Jr.
      3. Students and sit-ins
      4. CORE freedom rides
      5. Crisis at University of Mississippi
      6. Birmingham
      7. Wallace and the University of Alabama
      8. March on Washington
   D. Warren Court
      1. School prayer
      2. Rights of defendants

III. Kennedy and foreign affairs
   A. Early setbacks
      1. Bay of Pigs disaster
      2. Vienna summit
      3. Berlin
   B. Cuban missile crisis
      1. Causes of crisis

2. Kennedy's action
3. Resolution of crisis
4. Aftereffects
C. Vietnam
   1. Neutrality for Laos
   2. Problems with Diem
   3. Kennedy's reluctance to escalate
   4. Overthrow of Diem

IV. Assassination of President Kennedy
   A. Lee Harvey Oswald
   B. Warren Commission
   C. Continuing controversy

V. Lyndon Johnson and the Great Society
   A. Background and personality
   B. War on poverty
      1. *The Other America*
      2. 1964 tax cut
      3. Economic Opportunity Act
   C. Election in 1964
      1. Goldwater—choice not echo
      2. LBJ appeals to consensus
      3. Johnson landslide
   D. Landmark legislation
      1. Health insurance
      2. Aid to education
      3. Appalachian redevelopment
      4. Housing and urban development
   E. Shortcomings of Great Society

VI. From civil rights to black power
   A. Civil Rights Act of 1964
   B. Voting Rights Act of 1965
      1. The Selma march
      2. Provisions of the act

C. Development of black power
   1. Race riots of 1965 and 1966
   2. Plight of urban blacks
   3. Call for black power
      a. Stokely Carmichael
      b. Black Panther party
      c. Malcolm X
   4. Assessment of black power

VII. The tragedy of Vietnam
   A. Dimensions of war
      1. Troop commitments
      2. Cost of fighting
   B. Escalation
      1. Gulf of Tonkin Resolution
      2. Bombing and combat troops in 1965
   C. Context for policy
      1. Containment theory
      2. Not an accident
      3. Erosion of support for war
      4. Unity of North Vietnamese
   D. Turning point of the war
      1. Tet offensive
      2. Presidential primaries
      3. LBJ decides not to run

VIII. The crescendo of the sixties
   A. Assassinations in 1968
      1. Martin Luther King, Jr.
      2. Robert F. Kennedy
   B. Election of 1968
      1. Chicago and Miami
      2. George Wallace
      3. Election of Nixon

KEY ITEMS OF CHRONOLOGY

Kennedy administration	1961–63
Bay of Pigs invasion	April 1961
Freedom rides	May 1961
Cuban missile crisis	October 1963
Overthrow of Ngo Dinh Diem	November 1963
Kennedy assassination	November 22, 1963
Civil Rights Act (public accommodations)	July 1964
Gulf of Tonkin Resolution	August 1964
Voting Rights Act	1965
Tet offensive	January–February 1968
Assassinations of King and Robert Kennedy	1968

TERMS TO MASTER

Listed below are some important terms or people with which you should be familiar after you complete the study of this chapter. Explain the significance of each name or term.

1. New Frontier
2. Peace Corps
3. Martin Luther King, Jr.
4. SNCC
5. Freedom rides
6. Bay of Pigs invasion
7. Berlin Wall
8. Cuban missile crisis
9. Nuclear Test Ban Treaty
10. Ngo Dinh Diem
11. Great Society
12. *The Other America*
13. Medicare and Medicaid
14. Barry Goldwater
15. Watts riot
16. black power
17. Malcolm X
18. Gulf of Tonkin Resolution
19. Vietcong
20. Tet offensive
21. Eugene McCarthy
22. Robert Kennedy

VOCABULARY BUILDING

Listed below are some words used in this chapter. Look up each word in your dictionary.

1. trauma
2. pundits
3. chameleon
4. scurrilous
5. infidelity
6. desegregate
7. sublime
8. debacle
9. immolate
10. crescendo

EXERCISES FOR UNDERSTANDING

When you have completed the reading of the chapter, answer each of the following questions. If you have difficulty, go back and reread the section of the chapter related to the question.

Multiple-Choice Questions

Select the letter of the response that best completes the statement.

1. By 1960 John F. Kennedy had
   A. a long and distinguished political career.
   B. a great reputation as an able legislator.
   C. charm, good looks, wit, and wealth.
   D. all of the above

2. Congress blocked Kennedy's proposals for
   A. a tax cut.
   B. federal aid to education.
   C. health insurance for the elderly.
   D. all of the above

3. In the Cuban missile crisis, President Kennedy ordered
   A. surgical air strikes of Cuba.
   B. a quarantine of Cuba.
   C. the Bay of Pigs invasion.
   D. removal of U.S. missiles from Turkey.

4. By the end of 1963, the United States had sent to Vietnam
   A. only 2,000 military advisers.
   B. more than 15,000 military advisers.
   C. 25,000 fighting troops.
   D. over 100,000 fighting troops.

5. *The Other America* aroused concern about
   A. aid to South America.
   B. poverty.
   C. rights of blacks.
   D. the women's movement.

6. In 1964 Lyndon Johnson defeated
   A. Richard Nixon.
   B. Nelson Rockefeller.
   C. Barry Goldwater.
   D. Robert Taft.

7. Discrimination in hotels and restaurants was outlawed by

A. the Supreme Court's *Brown* decision in 1954.
B. Martin Luther King's "I Have a Dream" speech.
C. presidential order of Kennedy.
D. the Civil Rights Act of 1964.

8. Johnson sought to deescalate the Vietnam War because
A. the Tet offensive showed that the U.S. could not win.
B. political challengers showed the high level of public opposition to the war.
C. key national leaders called on him to end the war.
D. of all of the above

True-False Questions

Indicate whether each statement is true or false.

1. Nixon's 1960 campaign benefited from his televised debate with Kennedy.
2. Planning for the Bay of Pigs invasion began in the Eisenhower administration.
3. Kennedy supported neutrality for Laos.

4. The effects of the 1964 tax cut helped finance the war on poverty.
5. Goldwater opposed the nuclear test ban and the Civil Rights Act.
6. Martin Luther King, Jr., was the head of the SNCC.
7. The first American combat troops went to Vietnam in 1966.
8. The Tet offensive had a great effect on American public opinion.

Essay Questions

1. How did John Kennedy personify the "New Frontier"?
2. Assess the successes and failures of JFK's foreign policy.
3. Compare and contrast the achievements of the New Frontier and the Great Society.
4. What were the major milestones in the Vietnam conflict between 1961 and 1986?
5. How effective was the civil rights movement of the 1960s?
6. Account for the election of Richard Nixon in 1968.

DOCUMENT

Johnson's Speech on Vietnam, 1965

The speech that follows, given at Johns Hopkins University on April 7, 1965, contains President Johnson's rationale for a critical buildup of American forces in South Vietnam. That year, 1965, proved to be a fateful year for American involvement in Vietnam.

. . . Over this war, and all Asia, is the deepening shadow of Communist China. The rulers in Hanoi are urged on by Peking. This is a regime which has destroyed freedom in Tibet, attacked India, and been condemned by the United Nations for aggression in Korea. It is a nation which is helping the forces of violence in almost every continent. The contest in Vietnam is part of a wider pattern of aggressive purpose.

Why are these realities our concern? Why are we in South Vietnam? We are there because we have a promise to keep. Since 1954 every American President has offered support to the people of South Vietnam. We have helped to build, and we have helped to defend. Thus, over many years, we have made a national pledge to help South Vietnam defend its independence. And I intend to keep our promise.

To dishonor that pledge, to abandon this small and brave nation to its enemy, and to the terror that must follow, would be an unforgivable wrong.

We are also there to strengthen world order. Around the globe, from Berlin to Thailand, are people whose well-being rests, in part, on the belief that they can count on us if they are attacked. To leave Vietnam to its fate would shake the confidence of all these people in the value of American commitment, the value of America's word. The result would be increased unrest and instability, and even wider war.

We are also there because there are great stakes in the balance. Let no one think for a moment that retreat from Vietnam would bring an end to conflict. The battle would be renewed in one country and then another. The central lesson of our time is that the appetite of aggression is never satisfied. To withdraw from one battlefield means only to prepare for the next. We must say in Southeast Asia, as we did in Europe, in the words of the Bible: "Hitherto shalt thou come, but no further."

There are those who say that all our effort there will be futile, that China's power is such it is bound to dominate all Southeast Asia. But there is no end to that argument until all the nations of Asia are swallowed up.

There are those who wonder why we have a responsibility there. We have it for the same reason we have a responsibility for the defense of freedom in Europe. World War II was fought in both Europe and Asia, and when it ended we found ourselves with continued responsibility for the defense of freedom.

Our objective is the independence of South Vietnam, and its freedom from attack. We want nothing for ourselves, only that the people of South Vietnam be allowed to guide their own country in their own way.

We will do everything necessary to reach that objective. And we will do only what is absolutely necessary.

In recent months, attacks on South Vietnam were stepped up. Thus it became necessary to increase our response and to make attacks by air. This is not a change of purpose. It is a change in what we believe that purpose requires.

We do this in order to slow down aggression.

We do this to increase the confidence of the brave people of South Vietnam who have bravely borne this brutal battle for so many years and with so many casualties.

And we do this to convince the leaders of North Vietnam, and all who seek to share their conquest, of a very simple fact:

We will not be defeated.

We will not grow tired.

We will not withdraw, either openly or under the cloak of a meaningless agreement. . . .

Once this is clear, then it should also be clear that the only path for reasonable men is the path of peaceful settlement.

Such peace demands an independent South Vietnam securely guaranteed and able to shape its own relationships to all others, free from outside interference, tied to no alliance, a military base for no other country.

These are the essentials of any final settlement.

We will never be second in the search for such a peaceful settlement in Vietnam.

There may be many ways to this kind of peace: in discussion or negotiation with the governments concerned; in large groups or in small ones; in the reaffirmation of old agreements or their strengthening with new ones.

We have stated this position over and over again fifty times and more, to friend and foe alike. And we remain ready, with this purpose, for unconditional discussions.

And until that bright and necessary day of peace we will try to keep conflict from spreading. We have no desire to see thousands die in battle, Asians or Americans. We have no desire to devastate that which the people of North Vietnam have built with toil and sacrifice. We will use our power with restraint and with all the wisdom we can command. But we will use it. . . .

We will always oppose the effort of one nation to conquer another nation.

We will do this because our own security is at stake.

But there is more to it than that. For our generation has a dream. It is a very old dream. But we have the power and now we have the opportunity to make it come true.

For centuries, nations have struggled among each other. But we dream of a world where disputes are settled by law and reason. And we will try to make it so.

For most of history men have hated and killed one another in battle. But we dream of an end to war. And we will try to make it so.

For all existence most men have lived in poverty, threatened by hunger. But we dream of a world where all are fed and charged with hope. And we will help to make it so.

The ordinary men and women of North Vietnam and South Vietnam—of China and India—of Russia and America—are brave people. They are filled with the same proportions of hate and fear, of love and hope. Most of them want the same things for themselves and their families. Most of them do not want their sons ever to die in battle, or see the homes of others destroyed. . . .

Every night before I turn out the lights to sleep, I ask myself this question: Have I done everything that I can do to unite this country? Have I done everything I can to help unite the world, to try to bring peace and hope to all the peoples of the world? Have I done enough?

Ask yourselves that question in your homes and in this hall tonight. Have we done all we could? Have we done enough? . . .

[*Department of State Bulletin,* April 26, 1965 (Washington, D. C.: U. S. Government Printing Office, 1940–)]

Questions for Reflection

Compare Lyndon Johnson's address to Franklin Roosevelt's speech of January 1941 in Chapter 28. To what extent were they concerned about the same kinds of threats? Was Johnson correct in drawing parallels between events in Vietnam and events in Europe before World War II? What similarities and differences do you see? What is your view of the policy Johnson outlines here?

ANSWERS TO MULTIPLE-CHOICE
AND TRUE-FALSE QUESTIONS

Multiple-Choice Questions

1-C, 2-D, 3-B, 4-B, 5-B, 6-C, 7-D, 8-D

True-False Questions

1-F, 2-T, 3-T, 4-T, 5-T, 6-F, 7-F, 8-T

34

REBELLION AND REACTION
IN THE SEVENTIES

CHAPTER OBJECTIVES

After you complete the reading and study of this chapter you should be able to

1. Account for the rise and decline of New Left protests.
2. Describe the counterculture and its impact.
3. Trace the reform movements for women, Hispanics, Indians, and the environment.
4. Explain Nixon's aims in Vietnam.
5. Assess the impact of the Vietnam War on American society, military morale, and later foreign policy.
6. Explain Nixon's goals in domestic policy and account for his limited accomplishment.
7. Explain the problems plaguing the United States economy in the decade of the 1970s, and describe the various cures Nixon tried.
8. Describe Nixon's foreign policy triumphs in China and the Soviet Union, and explain their significance.
9. Discuss the Watergate coverup and account for the difficulty in unraveling it.
10. Describe the brief presidency of Gerald Ford.
11. Assess the Carter administration's successes and failures.

CHAPTER OUTLINE

I. Youth revolt
   A. Baby boomers as young adults
   B. Sit-ins and end of apathy

II. New Left
   A. Students for a Democratic Society
      1. Port Huron Statement
      2. Participatory democracy
   B. Free Speech movement
      1. Berkeley
      2. Quality of campus life
   C. Antiwar protests
   D. Growing militance
   E. 1968
      1. Columbia University uprising
      2. Democratic convention in Chicago
      3. Fracturing of SDS

III. Counterculture
   A. Descendants of the Beats
   B. Contrasted with New Left
   C. Drugs, communes, hedonism
   D. Rock music
      1. Woodstock
      2. Altamont

IV. Feminism
   A. Betty Friedan's *The Feminine Mystique*
   B. National Organization of Women

C. Federal actions
   1. Affirmative action
   2. *Roe v. Wade*
   3. Equal Rights Amendment's failure
D. Divisions and reactions

V. Minorities
  A. Hispanics
    1. United Farm Workers
    2. Chicanos, Puerto Ricans, Cubans
    3. Political power
  B. American Indians
    1. Emergence of Indian rights
    2. American Indian Movement
    3. Legal actions

VI. Gay rights
  A. Stonewall Inn raid
  B. Gay Liberation Front
  C. Gay rights movement

VII. "Silent majority"

VIII. Nixon and Vietnam
  A. The policy of gradual withdrawal
  B. Movement on three fronts
    1. Insistance on Communist withdrawal from South Vietnam
    2. Efforts to undercut unrest in the United States
      a. Troop reductions
      b. Lottery and volunteer army
    3. Expanded air war
  C. Occasions for public outcry against the war
    1. My Lai massacre
    2. Cambodian "incursion"
      a. Campus riots
      b. Public reaction
    3. *Pentagon Papers*
      a. Method of disclosure
      b. Revelations of the papers
      c. Supreme Court ruling
  D. American withdrawal
    1. Kissinger's efforts before the 1972 election
    2. The Christmas bombings
    3. Final acceptance of peace
    4. U.S. withdrawal in March 1973
  E. Ultimate victory of the North: March–April 1975
  F. Assessment of the war
    1. Communist control
    2. Failure to transfer democracy
    3. Erosion of respect for the military

    4. Drastic division of the American people
    5. Impact on future foreign policy

IX. Nixon and Middle America
  A. A reflection of Middle American values
  B. Domestic affairs
    1. Continuance of civil rights progress
      a. Voting Rights Act continued over a veto
      b. Courts uphold integration
        i. In Mississippi
        ii. School busing
        iii. Limitation on busing
        iv. The *Bakke* decision
    2. Revenue sharing
    3. Other domestic legislation
  C. The economic malaise
    1. The causes of stagflation
    2. Nixon's efforts to improve the economy
      a. Reducing the federal deficit
      b. Reducing the money supply
      c. Wage and price controls

X. Nixon's foreign triumphs
  A. Rapprochement with China
  B. Détente with the Soviet Union
    1. The visit to Moscow
    2. The SALT agreement
  C. Kissinger's shuttle diplomacy in the Middle East

XI. The election of 1972
  A. Removal of the Wallace threat
  B. The McGovern candidacy
  C. Results of the election

XII. Watergate
  A. Unraveling the coverup
    1. Judge Sirica's role
    2. Nixon's personal role
    3. April resignations
    4. Discovery of the tapes
    5. The Saturday Night Massacre
    6. The Court decides against the president
    7. Articles of impeachment
    8. The resignation
  B. The aftermath of Watergate
    1. Ford's selection
    2. The Nixon pardon
    3. Resiliency of American institutions

4. War Powers Act
5. Campaign financing legislation
6. Freedom of Information Act

XIII. An Unelected President
  A. Ford administration
    1. Drift at the end of Nixon administration
    2. Battle with the economy
    3. Diplomatic accomplishments
  B. Election of 1976
    1. Ford's nomination
    2. Rise of Jimmy Carter
    3. Carter's victory

XIV. Carter presidency
  A. Early domestic moves
    1. Appointments

2. Amnesty for draft dodgers
3. Environmental legislation
4. Energy crisis
5. Crisis of confidence
  B. Foreign policy initiatives
    1. Human rights
    2. Panama Canal treaties
    3. Camp David Agreement
  C. Troubles
    1. Stagflation
    2. SALT II Treaty
    3. Soviet invasion of Afghanistan
  D. Iranian crisis
    1. Background
    2. Efforts to aid hostages
    3. End of 444-day crisis

KEY ITEMS OF CHRONOLOGY

Port Huron Statement	1962
Betty Friedan's *The Feminine Mystique*	1963
NOW founded	1966
My Lai massacre	1968
Stonewall Inn riot	1969
Woodstock Music Festival	1969
Cambodian "incursion"	April 1970
Swann v. Charlotte-Mecklenburg Board of Education	1971
Pentagon Papers published	June 1971
Roe v. Wade	1972
Nixon's visit to China	February 1972
SALT agreement signed	May 1972
Watergate break-in occurred	June 1972
Last American troops left Vietnam	March 1973
War Powers Act	1973
Nixon's resignation	Aug. 9, 1974
South Vietnam fell to the North	April 1975
Bakke v. Board of Regents of California	1978

TERMS TO MASTER

Listed below are some important terms or people with which you should be familiar after you complete the study of this chapter. Explain the significance of each name or term.

1. New Left
2. SDS
3. participatory democracy
4. Free Speech movement
5. Weathermen
6. counterculture
7. Betty Friedan
8. NOW
9. Equal Rights Amendment
10. Gay Liberation Front
11. "silent majority"
12. *Pentagon Papers*

13. *Swann v. Charlotte-Mecklenburg Board of Education*
14. *Bakke v. Board of Regents of California*
15. revenue sharing
16. Spiro Agnew
17. OPEC
18. SALT
19. George McGovern
20. Watergate
21. Saturday Night Massacre
22. Henry Kissinger
23. War Powers Act

VOCABULARY BUILDING

Listed below are some words used in this chapter. Look up each word in your dictionary.

1. estranged
2. odious
3. nihilistic
4. mesmerize
5. hedonism
6. karma
7. assuage
8. poignant
9. ignoble
10. tenor
11. détente
12. lamentation
13. incriminating
14. impeach
15. rapprochment
16. carping
17. interregnum
18. effigy

EXERCISES FOR UNDERSTANDING

When you have completed reading the chapter, answer each of the following questions. If you have difficulty, go back and reread the section of the chapter related to the question.

Multiple-Choice Questions

Select the letter of the response that best completes the statement.

1. The leaders of the New Left included
   A. Tom Hayden and Mark Rudd.
   B. Abbie Hoffman and Cesar Chavez.
   C. Richard Daley and Spiro Agnew.
   D. Timothy Leary and Richie Havens.

2. Betty Friedan launched the women's movement with claims that women
   A. were too educated to dabble in politics.
   B. deserved equality with men in all areas.
   C. should be permitted to serve in the armed forces.
   D. were bored with housework and child care.

3. In *Roe v. Wade* the Supreme Court ruled that
   A. busing for school integration was unconstitutional.
   B. Indians were to receive four million acres in Wyoming.
   C. abortion in the first three months of pregnancy was legal.
   D. the Watergate coverup was sufficient to impeach Nixon.

4. The Stonewall Inn riot of 1969 involved
   A. free speech on college campuses.
   B. the Vietnam war.
   C. homosexual rights.
   D. none of the above.

5. Nixon sought to lessen criticism of the Vietnam War by
   A. slowly reducing the number of American troops there.
   B. creating a lottery to determine who would be drafted.
   C. using more air strikes rather than ground warfare.
   D. all of the above methods

6. During the Watergate crisis, Nixon was *not* accused of
   A. obstructing justice through paying witnesses to remain silent.
   B. defying Congress by withholding the tapes.
   C. using federal agencies to deprive citizens of their rights.

D. stealing funds from the reelection campaign.

7. Jimmy Carter's 1976 victory can be attributed to
   A. his strong support among southern blacks.
   B. the traditional Democratic sweep of the West.
   C. his long career as a national politician.
   D. the large voter turnout in the election.

8. Carter's most significant accomplishment in foreign policy was
   A. retaining complete control over the Panama Canal.
   B. an agreement with OPEC on oil prices.
   C. opposition to Soviet invasion of Afghanistan.
   D. a treaty between Israel and Egypt.

True-False Questions

Indicate whether each statement is true or false.

1. Campus turmoil in 1968 reached a peak at Columbia University.
2. The Cambodian "incursion" led to widespread rioting on American college campuses.
3. Two years after the Vietnam War ended, North Vietnam took control of the South.
4. Nixon used wage and price controls to stem inflation.
5. The War Powers Act requires a

president to withdraw troops sent abroad after sixty days unless Congress specifically authorizes a longer stay.
6. Gerald Ford called the fight against inflation "the moral equivalent of war."
7. Carter stressed a foreign policy of pragmatism rather than supporting a policy based on fixed principle.
8. The shah's secret police masterminded the seizure of Americans in Teheran in 1979.

Essay Questions

1. Compare and contrast the New Left and the counterculture.
2. Evaluate the accomplishments of the women's movement in the 1960s and 1970s.
3. How did Nixon's Vietnam War policies compare with Johnson's?
4. Discuss the impact of the Vietnam War on American society.
5. How did Nixon try to appeal to the "silent majority" with his domestic policies? Did he succeed?
6. How important were Nixon's diplomatic achievements with China and Russia? Could a Democrat have achieved the same gains? Explain.
7. Explain the Watergate controversy and Nixon's involvement in it.
8. What were the shortcomings and weaknesses of Jimmy Carter and his administration?

DOCUMENTS

Document 1. The Charges against Nixon

When the House Judiciary Committee completed its investigation and voted the impeachment of Nixon in July 1974, three articles obtained a majority vote of the committee. Those three articles are excerpted here.

> Article I. In his conduct of the office of President of the United States, Richard M. Nixon, in violation of his constitutional oath faithfully to execute the office of President of the United States and, to the best of his ability, preserve, protect, and defend the Constitution of the United States, and in violation of his constitutional duty

to take care that the laws be faithfully executed, has prevented, obstructed, and impeded the administration of justice, . . . Richard M. Nixon, using the powers of his high office, engaged personally and through his subordinates and agents, in a course of conduct or plan designed to delay, impede, and obstruct the investigation of such unlawful entry; to cover up, conceal and protect those responsible; and to conceal the existence and scope of other unlawful covert activities. . . .

Article II.   . . . Richard M. Nixon . . . has repeatedly engaged in conduct violating the constitutional rights of citizens, impairing the due and proper administration of justice and the conduct of lawful inquiries, or contravening the laws governing agencies of the executive branch and the purpose of these agencies. . . .

Article III. Richard M. Nixon, contrary to his oath faithfully to execute the office of President of the United States . . . has failed without lawful cause or excuse to produce papers and things as directed by duly authorized subpoenas issued by the Committee on the Judiciary of the House of Representatives on April 11, 1974, May 15, 1974, May 30, 1974, and June 24, 1974, and willfully disobeying such subpoenas. . . . In refusing to produce these papers and things, Richard M. Nixon, substituting his judgment as to what materials were necessary for the inquiry, interposed the powers of the Presidency against the lawful subpoenas of the House of Representatives, thereby assuming to himself functions and judgments necessary to the exercise of the sole power of impeachment vested by the Constitution in the House of Representatives.

[U.S. Congress, House of Representatives, *Report of the Committee on the Judiciary,* 93rd Cong., 2d sess., 1974.]

Document 2. Senator Sam Ervin Explains the Meaning and Consequences of Watergate

Prior to the report quoted above, the Ervin Committee of the Senate had throughout the summer of 1973 treated the American public to weeks of televised hearings at which various Watergate conspirators had testified about the labyrinthine developments of the Watergate affair. In June 1974, shortly before the House Judiciary Committee moved to impeach Nixon, the Ervin Committee made its report. Accompanying the report was a statement from Senator Ervin in which he tried to summarize the Watergate episode in a few paragraphs. Because the report was made prior to the House committee's decision to move toward impeachment of the president, Ervin began his report with a disclaimer to indicate that he was not trying to pass judgment on the president's guilt in the matter. His report is a succinct statement of the Watergate affair and a comment on its implications for the future.

I am not undertaking to usurp and exercise the power of impeachment, which the Constitution confers upon the House of Representatives alone. As a consequence, nothing I say should be construed as an expression of an opinion in respect to the question of whether or not President Nixon is impeachable in connection with the Watergate or any other matter. . . .

I shall also refrain from making any comment on the question of whether or not the President has performed in an acceptable manner his paramount constitutional obligation "to take care that the laws be faithfully executed."

Watergate was not invented by enemies of the Nixon administration or even by the news media. On the contrary, Watergate was perpetrated upon America by White House and political aides, whom President Nixon himself had entrusted with the management of his campaign for reelection to the Presidency, a campaign which was divorced to a marked degree from the campaigns of other Republicans who sought election to public office in 1972. I note at this point without elaboration that these White House and political aides were virtually without experience in either Government or politics apart from their association with President Nixon.

5. Watergate was without precedent in the political annals of America in respect to the scope and intensity of its unethical and illegal actions. To be sure, there had been previous milder political scandals in American history. That fact does not excuse Watergate. Murder and stealing have occurred in every generation since Earth began, but that fact has not made murder meritorious or larceny legal.

What Was Watergate?

Watergate was a conglomerate of various illegal and unethical activities in which various officers and employees of the Nixon reelection committee and various White House aides of President Nixon participated in varying ways and degrees to accomplish these successive objectives:

1. To destroy, insofar as the Presidential election of 1972 was concerned, the integrity of the process by which the President of the United States is nominated and elected.

2. To hide from law enforcement officers, prosecutors, grand jurors, courts, the news media, and the American people the identities and wrongdoing of those officers and employees of the Nixon reelection committees, and those White House aides who had undertaken to destroy the integrity of the process by which the President of the United States is nominated and elected.

To accomplish the first of these objectives. . . .

1. They exacted enormous contributions—usually in cash—from corporate executives by impliedly implanting in their minds the impressions that the making of the contributions was necessary to insure that the corporations would receive governmental favors, or avoid governmental disfavors, while President Nixon remained in the White House. A substantial portion of the contributions were made out of corporate funds in violation of a law enacted by Congress a generation ago.

2. They hid substantial parts of these contributions in cash in safes and safe deposits to conceal their sources and the identities of those who had made them.

3. They disbursed substantial portions of these hidden contributions in a surreptitious manner to finance the bugging and the burglary of the offices of the Democratic National Committee in the Watergate complex in Washington. . . .

4. They deemed the departments and agencies of the Federal Government to be the political playthings of the Nixon administration rather than impartial instruments for serving the people, and undertook to induce them to channel Federal contracts, grants, and loans to areas, groups, or individuals so as to promote the reelection of the President rather than to further the welfare of the people.

5. They branded as enemies of the President individuals and members of the news media who dissented from the President's policies and opposed his reelection, and conspired to urge the Department of Justice, the Federal Bureau of Investigation, the Internal Revenue Service, and the Federal Communications Commission to pervert the use of their legal powers to harass them for so doing.

6. They borrowed from the Central Intelligence Agency disguises which E. Howard Hunt used in political espionage operations, and photographic equipment which White House employees known as the "Plumbers" and their hired confederates used in connection with burglarizing the office of a psychiatrist which they believed contained information concerning Daniel Ellsberg which the White House was anxious to secure.

7. They assigned to E. Howard Hunt, who was at the time a White House consultant occupying an office in the Executive Office Building, the gruesome task of falsifying State Department documents which they contemplated using in their altered state to discredit the Democratic Party by defaming the memory of former President John Fitzgerald Kennedy, who as the hapless victim of an assassin's bullet had been sleeping in the tongueless silence of the dreamless dust for 9 years.

8. They used campaign funds to hire saboteurs to forge and disseminate false and scurrilous libels of honorable men running for the Democratic Presidential nomination in Democratic Party primaries.

During the darkness of the early morning of June 17, 1972, James W. McCord, the security chief of the John Mitchell committee, and four residents of Miami, Fla., were arrested by Washington police while they were burglarizing the offices of the Democratic National Committee in the Watergate complex to obtain political intelligence. . . .

The arrest of McCord and the four residents of Miami created consternation in the Nixon reelection committees and the White House. . . . various White House aides undertook to conceal from law enforcement officers, prosecutors, grand jurors, courts, the news media, and the American people the identities and activities of those officers and employees of the Nixon reelection committee and those White House aides who had participated in any way in the Watergate affair. . . .

1. They destroyed the records of the Nixon reelection committee antedating the bugging and the burglary.

2. They induced the Acting Director of the FBI, who was a Nixon appointee, to destroy the State Department documents which E. Howard Hunt had been falsifying.

3. They obtained from the Acting Director of the FBI copies of the scores of interviews conducted by the FBI agents in connection with their investigation of the bugging and the burglary, and were enabled thereby to coach their confederates to give false and misleading statements to the FBI.

4. They sought to persuade the FBI to refrain from investigating the sources of the campaign funds which were used to finance the bugging and the burglary.

5. They intimidated employees of the Nixon reelection committees and employees of the White House by having their lawyers present when these employees were being questioned by agents of the FBI, and thus deterred these employees from making full disclosures to the FBI.

6. They lied to agents of the FBI, prosecutors, and grand jurors who undertook to investigate the bugging and the burglary, and to Judge Sirica and the petit jurors who tried the seven original Watergate defendants in January, 1973.

7. They persuaded the Department of Justice and the prosecutors to take out-of-court statements from Maurice Stans, President Nixon's chief campaign fundraiser, and Charles Colson, Egil Krogh, and David Young, White House aides, and Charles Colson's secretary, instead of requiring them to testify before the grand jury investigating the bugging and the burglary in conformity with established procedures governing such matters, and thus denied the grand jurors the opportunity to question them.

8. They persuaded the Department of Justice and the prosecutors to refrain from asking Donald Segretti, their chief hired saboteur, any questions involving Herbert W. Kalmbach, the President's personal attorney, who was known by them to have paid Segretti for dirty tricks he perpetrated upon honorable men seeking the Democratic Presidential nomination. . . .

9. They made cash payments totaling hundreds of thousands of dollars out of campaign funds in surreptitious ways to the seven original Watergate defendants as hush money to buy their silence. . . .

10. They gave assurances to some of the original seven defendants that they would receive Presidential clemency after serving short portions of their sentences if they refrained from divulging the identities and activities of the officers and employees of the Nixon reelection committees and the White House aides who had participated in the Watergate affair.

11. They made arrangements by which the attorneys who represented the seven original Watergate defendants received their fees in cash from moneys which had been collected to finance President Nixon's reelection campaign.

12. They induced the Department of Justice and the prosecutors of the seven original Watergate defendants to assure the news media and the general public that there was no evidence that any persons other than the seven original Watergate defendants were implicated in any way in the Watergate-related crimes.

13. They inspired massive efforts on the part of segments of the news media friendly to the administration to persuade the American people that most of the members of the Select Committee

named by the Senate to investigate the Watergate were biased and irresponsible men motivated solely by desires to exploit the matters they investigated for personal or partisan advantage. . . .

One shudders to think that the Watergate conspiracies might have been effectively concealed and their most dramatic episode might have been dismissed as a "third-rate" burglary conceived and committed solely by the seven original Watergate defendants had it not been for the courage and penetrating understanding of Judge Sirica, the thoroughness of the investigative reporting of Carl Bernstein, Bob Woodward, and the other representatives of the free press, the labors of the Senate Select Committee and its excellent staff, and the dedication and diligence of Special Prosecutors Archibald Cox and Leon Jarworski and their associates.

Why Was Watergate?

Unlike the men who were responsible for Teapot Dome, the Presidential aides who perpetrated Watergate were not seduced by the love of money, which is sometimes thought to be the root of all evil. On the contrary, they were instigated by a lust for political power, which is at least as corrupting as political power itself. . . .

They knew that the power they enjoyed would be lost and the policies to which they adhered would be frustrated if the President should be defeated.

As a consequence of these things, they believed the President's reelection to be a most worthy objective, and succumbed to an age-old temptation. They resorted to evil means to promote what they conceived to be a good end.

Their lust for political power blinded them to ethical considerations and legal requirements; to Aristotle's aphorism that the good of man must be the end of politics; and to Grover Cleveland's conviction that a public office is a public trust.

They had forgotten, if they ever knew, that the Constitution is designed to be a law for rulers and people alike at all times and under all circumstances; and that no doctrine involving more pernicious consequences to the commonweal has ever been invented by the wit of man than the notion that any of its provisions can be suspended by the President for any reason whatsoever.

On the contrary, they apparently believed that the President is above the Constitution, and has the autocratic power to suspend its provisions if he decides in his own unreviewable judgment that his action in so doing promotes his own political interests or the welfare of the Nation. . . .

The Antidote for Future Watergates

Is there an antidote which will prevent future Watergates? If so, what is it? . . .

Candor compels the confession . . . that law alone will not suffice to prevent future Watergates. . . .

Law is not self-executing. Unfortunately, at times its execution rests in the hands of those who are faithless to it. And even when its enforcement is committed to those who revere it, law merely deters some human beings from offending, and punishes other human beings for offending. It does not make men good. This task can be performed only by ethics or religion or morality. . . .

When all is said, the only sure antidote for future Watergates is understanding of fundamental principles and intellectual and moral integrity in the men and women who achieve or are entrusted with governmental political power.

[U.S. Congress, Senate, Select Committee on Presidential Campaign Activities, *Final Report,* 93rd Cong., 2d sess., 1974, pp. 1097–1103]

Questions for Reflection

The United States Constitution in Article II, Section 4, states that the president "shall be removed from office on impeachment for, and on conviction of, treason, bribery, or other high crimes and misdemeanors." Do you consider the crimes of which Nixon was accused impeachable offenses? Why or why not?

Why was Ervin so careful to disavow any indictment of the president in his report? Based on the charges of the House Rules Committee in Document 1, which of the actions attributed to others by Ervin might have been charged to the president also?

Who benefited from the Watergate crimes? Were monetary considerations at the heart of the Watergate crimes? Is a president who is dutifully exercising his responsibilities "above the Constitution" with the power to suspend its provisions when he needs to do so? Explain.

What and/or who does Ervin credit with bringing the Watergate conspirators to justice? What does the case suggest about the need for an independent judiciary and a free press? How do you react to Ervin's prescription for preventing future Watergates?

ANSWERS TO MULTIPLE-CHOICE AND TRUE-FALSE QUESTIONS

Multiple-Choice Questions

1-A, 2-D, 3-C, 4-C, 5-D, 6-D, 7-A, 8-D

True-False Questions

1-T, 2-T, 3-T, 4-T, 5-T, 6-F, 7-T, 8-F

35

A NEW GILDED AGE

CHAPTER OBJECTIVES

1. Explain the popular appeal of Ronald Reagan.
2. Evaluate Ronald Reagan's economic policies.
3. Understand why commentators perceived the Reagan-Bush years as self-interested and greedy.
4. Discuss the U. S. role in Central America in the 1980s.
5. Assess the Iran-Contra affair.
6. Explain the economic difficulties of the Reagan-Bush era.
7. Describe the decline of communism in Europe in the late 1980s.
8. Discuss the causes and events of the Gulf War.
9. Understand the demographic changes highlighted by the 1990 census.

CHAPTER OUTLINE

I. Background of Reagan
  A. California
    1. Hollywood actor
    2. Spokesman for GE
    3. Liberal to conservative
    4. Conservative governor
  B. Political rise of Reagan

    1. Demographic changes
      a. Older population
      b. Growth of Sunbelt
    2. Religious revival
      a. Fundamentalism
      b. "Moral Majority"
      c. Traditional values
    3. Backlash against feminism
      a. Phyllis Schlafly and anti-ERA movement
      b. Anti-abortion movement
  C. Election of 1980
    1. Carter's decline
    2. Reagan's promises
    3. Reagan's victory
    4. Voter apathy
    5. Democrats' declining appeal

II. Reagan's first term
  A. Opulent inauguration
  B. Reaganomics
    1. Supply-side economics
    2. 1981 tax cut
    3. Budget cuts and deficits
    4. 1982 tax increase
  C. Conflicts of interests
  D. Effects of social policies
    1. Labor unions
    2. Feminism
    3. Minorities
  E. Foreign affairs in the 1980s
    1. Reagan's anti-communism

2. Military build-up
3. Emphasis on Central America
   a. El Salvador
   b. Nicaragua
     i. Sandinistas
     ii. Contras
4. Middle East
   a. Iran-Iraq war
   b. Lebanon, PLO, Israel
5. Grenada

III. Reagan's second term
  A. Election of 1984
    1. Economic recovery
    2. Mondale and taxes
    3. Landslide and its dangers
  B. Tax reform of 1986
  C. Arms control
    1. Obstacle of "Star Wars"
    2. Meetings with Gorbachev
  D. Decline in Reagan's popularity
    1. 1986 elections
    2. Revelations of "Irangate"
  E. Iran-Contra scandal
    1. Arms for hostages
    2. Profits to Contras
    3. North, Poindexter, McFarlane, Casey
    4. Congressional investigation
    5. Tower Commission
    6. Special prosecutor and indictments
  F. Troubles in Latin America
    1. Nicaraguan Contras
    2. Electoral defeat in El Salvador
    3. General Manuel Noriega in Panama
  G. Economic difficulties
    1. Soaring debt
    2. Stock market collapse
    3. Fear of recession
  H. INF agreement
  I. Reagan legacy

IV. The Bush years
  A. 1988 election
    1. Michael Dukakis
    2. George Bush
    3. Mud-slinging
    4. Results
  B. Tone of the Bush administration
  C. Domestic policies
    1. Economic problems
      a. Savings and loan crisis

      b. Budget deficits
      c. Tax increases and spending cuts
    2. Social issues
      a. AIDS
      b. Flag burning
      c. War on drug abuse
      d. The "underclass"
  D. Foreign affairs after the Cold War
    1. Democratic movements
      a. China
      b. Eastern Europe
      c. Soviet Union
      d. Mongolia
      e. Chile
      f. South Africa
    2. Dissolution of the Soviet Union
    3. Panama
      a. Manuel Noriega and drugs
      b. U. S. invasion
      c. Surrender of Noriega
  E. The Gulf War
    1. Iraq-Kuwait tension
    2. Iraq invasion of Kuwait
    3. U. N. resolutions 661 and 678
    4. "Desert Shield"
    5. Congressional debate
    6. "Desert Storm"
    7. Cease-fire
    8. Civil war
    9. American public reaction
  F. Nomination of Clarence Thomas
    1. Thomas's background
    2. Bush's support
    3. Anita Hill's charges of sexual harassment
    4. Senate Judiciary Committee hearing
    5. Senate confirmation
    6. Aftermath
  G. Economic recession
    1. Shrinkage of work force
    2. Excessive debt
    3. Low investment rate
    4. Response of Federal Reserve Board
  H. Election of 1992
    1. Anti-government sentiment of 1991 election
    2. Buchanan's challenge to Bush
    3. Rise of Bill Clinton
    4. Ross Perot

V. The nation in the 1990s
   A. Demographic changes
      1. An aging population
      2. Shift to the South and West
      3. Urbanization
      4. Working women
      5. Decline of family unit
      6. Black poverty
   B. New immigrants

      1. Illegal immigration
      2. Visa lottery
      3. Asian-Americans
      4. Mexicans
      5. Ethnic enclaves
      6. Effects
         a. Cultural pluralism
         b. New nativism and ethnic strife
   C. Racial conflict and Los Angeles riot

KEY ITEMS OF CHRONOLOGY

Reagan presidency	1981–1989
Economic Recovery Tax Act	August 1981
Attack on U. S. Marines in Beirut	October 1983
Invasion of Grenada	October 1983
Explosion of the *Challenger*	January 1986
Tax Reform Act	September 1986
Stock market plunge	October 1987
INF Treaty	December 1987
Tiananmen Square demonstrations	June 1989
Fall of the Berlin Wall	November 1989
Iraq invades Kuwait	August 1990
Desert Storm	January–February 1991
Parts of former Soviet Union becomes Commonwealth of Independent States	December 1991

TERMS TO MASTER

1. "Moral Majority"
2. stagflation
3. Reaganomics
4. "boll weevils"
5. contras
6. sleaze factor
7. Walter Mondale
8. Strategic Defense Initiative
9. Iran-Contra affair
10. Lieutenant-Colonel Oliver North
11. Tower Commission
12. AIDS
13. yuppies
14. Resolution Trust Corporation
15. *perestroika*
16. *glasnost*
17. Mikhail Gorbachev
18. Boris Yeltsin
19. Manuel Noriega
20. Saddam Hussein
21. Desert Shield
22. Desert Storm
23. Clarence Thomas
24. Anita Hill
25. Patrick Buchanan
26. Ross Perot

VOCABULARY BUILDING

1. enamored
2. fervid
3. demographic
4. opulence
5. euphemism
6. malevolent
7. reminiscent
8. incriminating
9. bravura

10. reverberate
11. scurrilous
12. patina
13. rancorous
14. intractable
15. apocalyptic
16. euphoria
17. doldrums
18. intractable

EXERCISES FOR UNDERSTANDING

Multiple-Choice Questions

1. In 1983, the U.S. military successfully invaded
   A. Iraq.
   B. El Salvador.
   C. Grenada.
   D. Lebanon.

2. The Iran-Contra affair involved
   A. selling arms for hostages in Iran.
   B. Lieutenant-Colonel Oliver North.
   C. secretly supporting rebels in Nicaragua.
   D. all of the above

3. The savings and loan crisis was caused by
   A. excessive regulation by the government.
   B. high-risk investments other than residential real estate.
   C. low inflation and falling interest rates.
   D. the stock market crash.

4. In 1987, Reagan signed a treaty with Gorbachev
   A. restricting biological and chemical warfare.
   B. eliminating intermediate-range nuclear weapons.
   C. ending the controversy over Afghanistan.
   D. settling the dispute between Israel and Lebanon.

5. In fighting Iraq in "Desert Storm," the Bush administration
   A. had the support of the United Nations in resolution 678.
   B. used 400,000 American troops.
   C. was assisted by forces from more than twenty other nations.

D. all of the above

6. One major effect of the Clarence Thomas-Anita Hill controversy was
   A. the defeat of Thomas.
   B. a resurgence in feminism.
   C. the impeachment of Hill.
   D. all of the above

7. "The Cold War is behind us now. Let us not wrangle over who won it," said
   A. Ronald Reagan.
   B. Ross Perot.
   C. George Bush.
   D. Mikhail Gorbachev.

8. In the 1980s, the single leading source of legal new immigrants to the United States was
   A. Mexico.
   B. China.
   C. Europe.
   D. Canada.

True-False Questions

1. One leader of the backlash against feminism was Phyllis Schlafly.
2. On October 19, 1987, the Dow Jones Industrial Average soared in response to the successful invasion of Grenada.
3. The income of the lowest 10 percent of American families stayed the same between 1977 and 1987.
4. In the White House, President Bush replaced Truman's picture with one of Coolidge.
5. The U.S. invaded Panama in 1989 to help Manuel Noriega.
6. The fastest-growing segment of the American population in the 1980s was Asian Americans.
7. The United States rate of investment is double the Japanese rate.
8. Ross Perot formed a third party to run for president in 1992.

Essay Questions

1. What factors contributed to the rise and success of Ronald Reagan before the the 1980 election?
2. What was "Reaganomics"? Describe its successes and failures.

3. Explain why some people consider the
   Reagan-Bush administrations a time of
   greed and corruption throughout
   American life.
4. Why was the "Iran-Contra affair"
   significant?
5. Where did democratic movements
   emerge after the end of the Cold War?

Assess their significance.
6. Describe the background of the Gulf
   War of 1990–1991.
7. Who were the new immigrants to the
   United States in the 1980s and what
   effects did they have on society?
8. What were the successes and
   shortcomings of the Bush administration?

DOCUMENT

**In his State of the Union address in 1985, President Ronald Reagan called
for a "Second American Revolution."**

My fellow citizens, this Nation is poised for greatness. The time has
come to proceed toward a great new challenge—a Second American Revolution of hope and opportunity; a revolution carrying us to
new heights of progress by pushing back frontiers of knowledge and
space; a revolution of spirit that taps the soul of America, enabling
us to summon greater strength than we have ever known; and, a
revolution that carries beyond our shores the golden promise of
human freedom in a world at peace.

Let us begin by challenging our conventional wisdom: There are
no constraints on the human mind, no walls around the human
spirit, no barriers to our progress except those we ourselves erect.
Already, pushing down tax rates has freed our economy to vault
forward to record growth. . . .

We stand on the threshold of a great ability to produce more, do
more, be more. Our economy is not getting older and weaker, it is
getting younger and stronger. It doesn't need rest and supervision,
it needs new challenge and greater freedom. And that word, *freedom,* is the key to the Second American Revolution that we mean
to bring about.

Let us move together with a historic reform of tax simplification
for fairness and growth. . . .

One thing that tax reform will not be is a tax increase in disguise.
We will not jeopardize the mortgage interest deduction that families need. We will reduce personal tax rates as low as possible by
removing many tax preferences. We will propose a top rate of not
more than 35 percent, and possibly lower. And we will propose
reducing corporate rates while maintaining incentives for capital
formation.

To encourage opportunity and jobs rather than dependency and
welfare, we will propose that individuals living at or near the poverty line be totally exempt from Federal income tax. To restore
fairness to families, we will propose increasing significantly the personal exemption. . . .

Tax simplification will be a giant step toward unleashing the tremendous pent-up power of our economy. But a Second American
Revolution must carry the promise of opportunity for all. It is time

to liberate the spirit of enterprise in the most distressed areas of our country.

This Government will meet its responsibility to help those in need. But policies that increase dependency, break up families, and destroy self-respect are not progressive, they are reactionary. Despite our strides in civil rights, blacks, Hispanics, and all minorities will not have full and equal power until they have full economic power.

We have repeatedly sought passage of enterprize zones to help those in the abandoned corners of our land find jobs, learn skills, and build better lives. . . .

Nor must we lose the chance to pass our Youth Employment Opportunity Wage proposal. We can help teenagers who have the highest unemployment rate find summer jobs, so they know the pride of work, and have confidence in their futures.

We will continue to support the Job Training Partnership Act, which has a nearly two-thirds job placement rate. Credits and education and health care vouchers will help working families shop for services they need.

Our Administration is already encouraging certain low-income public housing residents to own and manage their own dwellings. It is time that all public housing residents have that opportunity of ownership.

The Federal Government can help create a new atmosphere of freedom. But States and localities, many of which enjoy surpluses from the recovery, must not permit their tax and regulatory policies to stand as barriers to growth.

Let us resolve that we will stop spreading dependency and start spreading opportunity; that we will stop spreading bondage and start spreading freedom.

There are some who say that growth initiatives must await final action on deficit reductions. Well, the best way to reduce deficits is through economic growth. More businesses will be started, more investments made, more jobs created, and more people will be on payrolls paying taxes. The best way to reduce Government spending is to reduce the need for spending by increasing prosperity. . . .

To move steadily toward a balanced budget we must also lighten Government's claim on our total economy. We will not do this by raising taxes. We must make sure that our economy grows faster than the growth in spending by the Federal Government. . . . And three points are key:

First, the social safety net for the elderly, the needy, the disabled, and unemployed will be left intact. Growth of our major health care programs, Medicare and Medicaid, will be slowed, but protections for the elderly and needy will be preserved.

Second, we must not relax our efforts to restore military strength just as we near our goal of a fully equipped, trained, and ready professional corps. National security is Government's first responsibility, so, in past years, defense spending took about half the Federal budget. Today it takes less than a third. . . .

Third, we must reduce or eliminate costly Government subsidies. For example, deregulation of the airline industry has led to cheaper airfares, but on Amtrak taxpayers pay about $35 per passenger

every time an Amtrak train leaves the station. It's time we ended
this huge Federal subsidy.

Our farm program costs have quadrupled in recent years. . . . we
need an orderly transition to a market-oriented farm economy. We
can help farmers best, not by expanding Federal payments, but by
making fundamental reforms, keeping interest rates heading down,
and knocking down foreign trade barriers to American farm ex-
ports.

We are moving ahead with Grace Commission reforms to
eliminated waste, and improve Government's management practices. . . .

Nearly 50 years of Government living beyond its means has
brought us to a time of reckoning, Ours is but a moment in history.
But one moment of courage, idealism, and bipartisan unity can
change American history forever. . . .

Reducing unneeded red tape and regulations, and deregulating
the energy, transportation, and financial industries, have unleashed
new competition, giving consumers more choices, better services,
and lower prices.

We seek to fully deregulate natural gas to bring on new supplies
and bring us closer to energy independence. Consistent with safety
standards, we will continue removing restraints on the bus and
railroad industries; we will soon send up legislation to return Con-
rail to the private sector, where it belongs; and we will support
further deregulation of the trucking industry. . . .

Our Second American Revolution will push on to new possibilities
not only on Earth, but in the next frontier of space. Despite budget
restraints, we will seek record funding for research and development.

We have seen the success of the space shuttle. Now we are going
to develop a permanently manned Space Station, and new opportunities for free enterprise because in the next decade Americans
and our friends around the world will be living and working together in space. . . .

As we do all this; we will continue to protect our natural resources. We will seek reauthorization and expanded funding for the
Superfund program, to continue cleaning up hazardous waste sites
which threaten human health and the environment. . . . no citizen
should tremble, nor the world shudder, if a child stands in a class-
room and breathes a prayer. We ask you again—give children back
a right they had for a century and a half or more in this country.

The question of abortion grips our Nation. Abortion is either the
taking of a human life or it isn't; and if it is—and medical technology
is increasingly showing it is—it must be stopped. I ask you in the
Congress to move this year on legislation to protect the unborn.

In the area of education, we are returning to excellence and again
the heroes are our people, not government. We are stressing basics
of discipline, rigorous testing, and homework, while helping children become computer smart as well.

We must go forward in our commitment to the new basics, giving
parents greater authority and making sure good teachers are re-
warded for hard work and achievement through merit pay.

But we must do more. I urge proposals permitting use of all

reliable evidence that police officers acquire in good faith. These proposals would also reform the habeus corpus laws and allow, in keeping with the will of the overwhelming majority of Americans, the use of the death penalty where necessary.

There can be no economic revival in ghettos when the most violent among us are allowed to roam free. It is time we restored domestic tranquility. And we mean to do just that.

[From *Congressional Record*, 6 February 1985]

QUESTIONS FOR REFLECTION

What were the key points in Reagan's proposed "second American revolution"? In what ways were they genuinely revolutionary? Do you think Reagan's ideas were wise, practical, sensible? Did he succeed in bringing about the revolution? What effects did his policies have on the United States?

ANSWERS TO MULTIPLE-CHOICE AND TRUE-FALSE QUESTIONS

Multiple-Choice Questions

1-C, 2-D, 3-B, 4-B, 5-D, 6-B, 7-D, 8-A

True-False Questions

1-T, 2-F, 3-F, 4-F, 5-F, 6-T, 7-F, 8-F